Warrior
Treasure

Warrior Treasure

The Staffordshire Hoard in Anglo-Saxon England

Chris Fern and Jenni Butterworth

Published by Liverpool University Press on behalf of Historic England, The Engine House, Fire Fly Avenue, Swindon SN2 2EH
www.HistoricEngland.org.uk

Historic England is a Government service championing England's heritage and giving expert, constructive advice.

The views contained in this book are those of the authors alone and not Historic England or Liverpool University Press.

First published 2022

ISBN: 978-1-80085-481-9 paperback

British Library Cataloguing in Publication data
A CIP catalogue record for this book is available from the British Library.

Typeset in Charter 9/11

Page layout by Carnegie Book Production

Printed and bound by Gomer Press, Llandysul, Wales

Front cover: The reconstruction of the Staffordshire Hoard helmet
[© The Birmingham Museums Trust]

Contents

Acknowledgements

This book could not have been written about the Staffordshire Hoard without the scientific, conservation and research project that took place between 2011 and 2018, funded by the city councils of Birmingham and Stoke-on-Trent, Birmingham Museums Trust, The Potteries Museum & Art Gallery, Stoke-on-Trent, and Historic England, with other patrons. Thanks is due to all of them, as well as to project managers, Barbican Research Associates, for their support for the research project and this book.

That we have learnt so much about the collection since its discovery is a tribute to the hard work and close collaboration demonstrated by all the organisations and individuals who have worked on its research and conservation.

Abbreviations

Numbers next to objects in **bold** refer to their Staffordshire Hoard catalogue number: the catalogue is available online at https://doi.org/10.5284/1041576.

References to Bede's *Ecclesiastical History of the English People* are given as 'HE' with book and chapter number (eg HE II, 13).

Where Hoard is capitalised in the text, it refers to the Staffordshire Hoard specifically.

Introduction

The Staffordshire Hoard is the largest collection of precious-metal artefacts ever discovered from early Anglo-Saxon England, as well as a great archaeological mystery. Found in a farmer's field near Lichfield in 2009, the breathtaking trove of over 600 objects captured headlines worldwide. They amount to nearly 6kg of gold and silver, with many having glittering, blood-red garnet decoration, or other intricate ornament, and included are some of the finest examples of Anglo-Saxon craftsmanship known. The numerous parts come mainly from swords and other war gear, raising the tantalising prospect that they must relate in some way to the cycle of conflict that history records across 7th-century Britain, as rival pagan and Christian kingdoms fought for supremacy. Now, following more than a decade of research, the Hoard has started to give up its secrets, allowing key questions to be considered: how did the golden ornaments come together, where were they made, what happened to their noble owners, who might have owned and buried them, never to return, and when did it all happen?

We believe that the Hoard was buried around the mid-7th century AD, over 200 years after the end of Roman rule in Britain. A patchwork of early Anglo-Saxon kingdoms then existed in the eastern part of the British mainland, some with names still familiar today, such as Kent and East Anglia. Legends and early histories tell that the Anglo-Saxon territories were founded and settled from the 5th century onwards by waves of migrating groups from northern Europe, while in the west and north,

The Staffordshire Hoard.
[Birmingham Museums Trust]

I

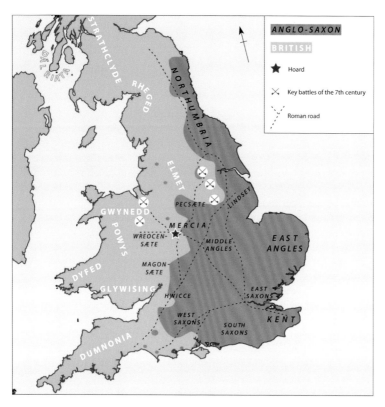

Anglo-Saxon England, showing the Staffordshire Hoard findspot.

[C Fern]

British and Romano-British communities remained and resisted. The Hoard is also contemporary with the great royal burial that took place at Sutton Hoo (Suffolk), that other most famous of discoveries from the early Anglo-Saxon period (5th to 7th centuries AD).

The field where the Hoard was found lay in what was a border territory in the 7th century, a region at the meeting point of Anglo-Saxon and British cultures. This was one of the last areas to take stable political form during the period, eventually becoming the kingdom of Mercia, and its rulers were also among the last to convert to Christianity, doing so at around the time the Hoard was buried. Nevertheless, the kingdom would ultimately achieve supreme power in the 8th century.

The objects of the Hoard are not all of one date and certainly some were antiques when they became part of the collection. Nonetheless, most of the assemblage was probably accrued over only a few decades, during the first half of the 7th century, a time which saw the rise of Mercia from a regional backwater at the end of the 6th century to a kingdom that could exert wide dominance 50 years later. From the account of the Anglo-Saxon historian Bede, written a century later, it is clear that key to this ascendancy was the series of successful military campaigns fought by King Penda of Mercia (d AD 655).

The finds that make up the Staffordshire Hoard, therefore, span a time of crucial change for Mercia and the British Isles in general, a half-century during which kingdoms faced triumph or defeat, and in which the institution of the growing English Church and Christianity came to eclipse the paganism of previous generations. Each object in the collection is a small physical record of this time, of a golden yet bloody age. The Hoard shows us the high arts of Anglo-Saxon England at their pinnacle, infused with meaning, but in the end as destroyed and concealed fragments. Each has a story to tell, starting with its manufacture by a smith, to its owner, whether warrior, prince or bishop, set against a landscape and society in flux as peoples and kingdoms fought, fell and were renewed under the Christian banner.

Discovery and investigation

'You have found me at last'

For Terry Herbert, the 5 July 2009 started out as a day much like any other. It was sunny, with a gentle breeze, and he headed out to enjoy his hobby of metal detecting for a few hours. The field he chose was one he'd driven past many times. Situated next to the major A5 road, near Lichfield, it wasn't the most promising site for detecting; nonetheless he'd asked permission to explore the field from the owner, farmer Fred Johnson. On his first attempt he found nothing more exciting than an 18th-century penny.

Then Terry found something unusual. At first, he thought it might be a brass fitting from modern furniture or jewellery, but closer inspection showed it was gold. Within just a few minutes, he'd found other gold objects, and although he wasn't sure what they were, he knew they were special. That night he was anxious about the importance of what he had discovered, and over the following days he found much more. In an interview later, Terry recalled what had kept repeating in his mind: 'You have found me at last'.

In England and Wales, finds that are of gold and silver, as well as groups of coins over 300 years old and some other assemblages, must be reported to the authorities under the 1996 Treasure Act. The Portable Antiquities Scheme (PAS), which operates regionally and is run centrally by the British Museum, provides a simple way for finders in England to

Eye-shaped mount **543**, showing how close to the surface some of the objects were lying when they were discovered.
[Staffordshire County Council]

report treasure and other archaeological discoveries. Terry reported his find to the PAS officer for the Staffordshire region, and subsequently Staffordshire County Council and Historic England organised an archaeological investigation at the site. Because the location was clearly visible from the busy A5 road, it was important to recover any remaining finds and archaeological evidence quickly, to guard against theft. Stories were required to keep the real purpose a secret, with passers-by and journalists given only the half-truth that 'no Roman pottery had been found yet'.

Treasure

Once safely recovered, the finds were catalogued by Kevin Leahy, an expert on Anglo-Saxon finds within the PAS. He identified 1,662 items, which included both single finds and groups of fragments still clumped together in soil. The case was then presented to the local coroner, an ancient institution in England, Wales and Northern Ireland, a regional public official with authority to adjudicate a range of matters. On 24 September 2009, the South Staffordshire coroner examined the evidence and duly declared the items on Kevin's list to be 'Treasure'.

The discovery immediately became headline news around the world. Basic information about the find was already clear: it was Anglo-Saxon, comprised hundreds of exceptional objects almost wholly made of precious metal, including fittings from weapons, and could be dated approximately to the 7th century AD. Some were similar in style and quality to extraordinary finds made in contemporary cemeteries elsewhere in England, most notably Sutton Hoo (Suffolk), having beautiful cloisonné inlaid with garnets and glass, or delicate gold wire filigree ornament. Many pieces carried animal art designs, inhabited by stylised birds, serpents and other beasts.

Each Hoard object or group of objects was assigned a unique 'K' (Kevin Leahy) number using raffle tickets. [Birmingham Museums Trust]

Sutton Hoo

This famous site near Woodbridge (Suffolk) was first excavated in 1939 by Basil Brown, and despite past grave robbing, excavations then and since have revealed a series of barrow or mound burials dated between the late 6th and mid-7th centuries AD. So impressive are the grave goods that it is generally accepted that it must have been a royal burial ground. Mound 1 contained a burial in a ship, with magnificent objects including a helmet, gold and garnet weaponry and other regalia, a sceptre, mail armour, silver feasting equipment, purse of coins and a great gold buckle. Some scholars believe that the burial was that of King Rædwald of East Anglia (d *c* AD 624), who was also for a time overlord of all the kingdoms south of the River Humber. Investigations by Professor Martin Carver in 1983–93 made new discoveries, such as the double burial of a young warrior and his horse under Mound 17. A contemporary royal settlement site is known from nearby Rendlesham, with archaeological survey (2009–2014) revealing an extensive and wealthy complex with evidence for high-status living, metalworking, and links to trade networks that stretched across Europe and the Mediterranean.

Sutton Hoo shoulder clasps.

The Hoard astounded experts and the public alike. The hundreds of gold pommels and other fittings from swords and fighting knives (seaxes) that dominate the collection illustrate a high warrior culture unlike anything seen before for the period. The king's burial in Mound 1 at Sutton Hoo provides one of the few comparable swords with gold fittings from Anglo-Saxon England. Now such similar treasures had, according to the finder, come out of the ground 'like potatoes' in the field in Staffordshire. In quantity, the nearly 6kg of precious metal of the Hoard is considerably greater by mass than the gold regalia and coins of the Sutton Hoo burial at 1.7kg, while the rare example of a gold coin and jewellery hoard from Crondall (Hampshire) found in 1828 was only 131g. Some of the most eye-catching of the finds are of a different character, however, being not obviously military but religious, the like of which were equally unknown. They include a large gold cross (**539**), a gold strip (**540**) with a Latin inscription, and a strange headdress (**541**) ornament. Almost immediately, speculation began about possible links between the Hoard and specific events known from the history of Bede.

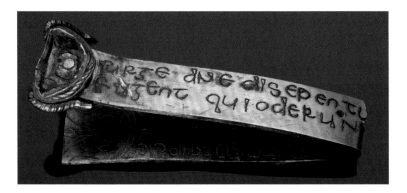

Gold strip **540** with Latin inscriptions on both sides.
[Birmingham Museums Trust]

Bede and the *Ecclesiastical History*

Bede (*c* AD 673–735) was a monk at the Northumbrian twin monastery of Monkwearmouth-Jarrow (Northumberland) and author of the *Historia ecclesiastica gentis Anglorum* (*The Ecclesiastical History of the English People*), our most important historical source for the early Anglo-Saxon period.

His pious history used largely Northumbrian sources and was written in part to celebrate the Christian deeds of the kings of his native kingdom. Accounts of good Christian rule and actions serve as exemplars for the reader, though the history also preserves some memories of pagan belief and practice. In one famous episode, Bede tells of the dramatic conversion of the pagan high priest Coifi (HE II, 13). Upon his acceptance of Christianity, he first mounts a stallion and takes up arms, trappings forbidden to a priest of the pagan religion we are told. Then he sets about destroying the temple of his old idols at Goodmanham (Yorkshire).

Northumbrian kings in the time of the Staffordshire Hoard, Edwin (AD 616–33), Oswald (AD 634–42) and Oswiu (AD 642–70), are especially celebrated for their devoutness. Bede's account of their campaigns against Penda (d AD 655), pagan king of the rival kingdom of Mercia, provides an evocative backdrop for the time period when the Hoard objects were made, used and buried.

Members of the public queuing at
Birmingham Museum to see the
first display in 2009.
[Birmingham Museums Trust]

The Hoard was discovered at the heart of the modern West Midlands. Local people felt very strongly that the find should remain within the region, so after it was valued at an enormous £3.285 million – the largest ever UK treasure case – initiatives were begun to achieve this. Two local city councils, Birmingham and Stoke-on-Trent, wished to jointly display the Hoard at Birmingham Museum & Art Gallery and at The Potteries Museum & Art Gallery, and they were given four months to raise sufficient funds to compensate the finder and the landowner, and so acquire the collection. The museums were supported by the Art Fund, other organisations and the public, and to everyone's surprise the money was raised with time to spare. Local and national support for the campaign was overwhelming, with tens of thousands of people queueing for hours to see the find and give donations. Indeed, the archaeological treasure became the largest public giving campaign of its kind, and this extraordinary generosity meant the collection was acquired by the two museums in June 2010.

Investigating the site

As the museums prepared to exhibit the treasure, archaeologists continued to explore the field where it had been discovered. The Hoard had been buried on a hilltop beside the Roman road of Watling Street (now the A5), near the village of Hammerwich.

All of the Hoard finds were discovered within the topsoil, indicating that they must have been deposited in a shallow pit or other feature subsequently destroyed by ploughing. In fact, no archaeology of contemporary or earlier date was found to suggest occupation or burial on the site, and a further investigation in 2010 added little more to this picture of isolation. It was shown, however, that a geological feature of glacial origin existed at the findspot. This might once have formed a landscape protuberance or lump that supported distinctive vegetation, and this perhaps could have served as a focus for the placing of the Hoard.

Unfortunately, Terry didn't record precise locations for the objects he recovered, but the archaeologists did plot those they excavated

Archaeologists at work in 2009 excavating the Hoard findspot, with the finder with his metal detector.
[University of Birmingham]

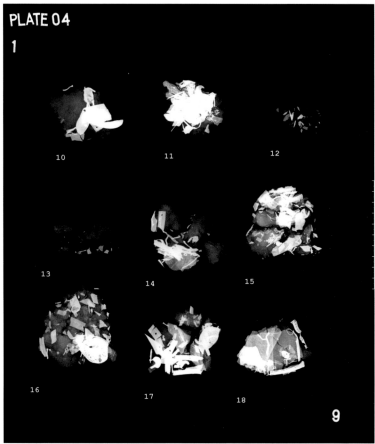

Some of the 'soil blocks' with X-ray showing silver fragments and gold objects inside.
[Courtesy of National Museums Liverpool (World Museum)]

Hoard objects found in 2012. The cheekpiece is more damaged than the one found in 2009, probably due to the additional plough action it was subjected to.
[Staffordshire County Council]

according to 1m × 1m grid squares. From this partial distribution, it can be suggested that the collection was buried within a 3–4m square area, from which it was spread by the plough to cover an area roughly 16m × 14m. Terry also discovered more than 20 'soil blocks' in a 2m × 2m area that subsequently proved to contain many tiny metal fragments, and it is possible these represent material that had settled at the bottom of a pit. No more precise information about the nature of the deposit is known.

In 2012, the farmer decided to plough the field to plant a potato crop. There had also been reports of suspicious activity on the site, possibly due to illegal metal detecting. Staffordshire County Council thus arranged for archaeologists to conduct a field survey using metal detectors, and 81 new fragments were discovered, including a helmet cheekpiece that was the pair to one found in 2009. The finds were valued at £57,395, a sum generously met by Wartski, the jewellers, allowing the museums to acquire these new items to join the rest of the collection. Additionally, two fragments from an early Anglo-Saxon horse-harness mount (**698**) were found some 40m from the main Hoard findspot, which joined another fragment also found in the field in 2009. The final object in the Hoard catalogue (but not actually or legally part of the same treasure), this mount has decoration related to other fittings in the collection and represents important evidence for activity on the site that is closely contemporary.

2 Conservation and research

Understanding the Hoard

Conservation and research began immediately once the collection had been secured by the two museums. The Hoard isn't a large collection when compared to many archaeological archives, but it did present specific challenges. Although it was probably a single assemblage before it was ploughed up, there was very little associated archaeological evidence to help researchers understand it. No evidence for settlements or other substantial activity had been found in the vicinity. Moreover, many objects were in fragments, caused by deliberate destruction prior to burial or due to deterioration in the ground. However, the near pristine decoration on many objects showed that the finds from 2009 had not suffered from repeated turning by the plough. Almost without exception, therefore, the finds required scrupulous and time-consuming attention in the laboratory. On top of this, the public interest in the collection meant that the museums had committed to keeping the collection on display as much as possible throughout the process, which sometimes meant that prior to reconstruction, fragments from a single object were in more than one location.

The archaeological research and conservation programme (2012–18) was one of the most complex and costly ever undertaken, funded by the museums and Historic England, with additional generous support from other patrons. A cohort of museum staff, students and volunteers, along with over 20 experts (archaeologists, art historians, conservators, historians and scientists) participated in the investigation of the remarkable find.

Mount **464** during the cleaning process.
[Birmingham Museums Trust]

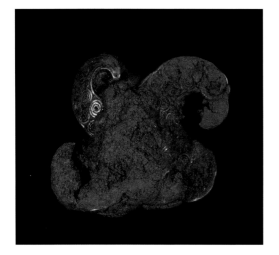
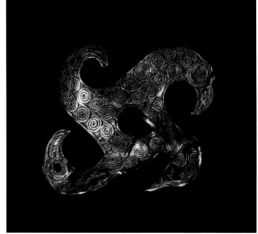

Revealing and recording

When first acquired, the objects were still soil-covered and bagged as they had been at discovery. The initial task of the investigative conservation was therefore to carefully clean each item, to reveal form and decoration, as well as to ascertain how stable the objects were and if they needed physical consolidation and supportive packaging to protect them. Natural thorns were used to remove soil instead of metal tools, as these would not scratch the soft gold. Most of the artefacts are small and have fine detail, so cleaning was conducted under a microscope, the soil being first dampened with distilled water, then carefully removed in small increments and retained as part of the archive. For some cloisonné-decorated items, full cleaning threatened the loss of loose garnets, so some soil was left in position.

The Hoard conservation team at Birmingham Museum.
[Birmingham Museums Trust]

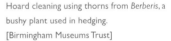

Hoard cleaning using thorns from *Berberis*, a bushy plant used in hedging.
[Birmingham Museums Trust]

Cloisonné

There are 131 objects with cloisonné ornament, each of painstaking and miniature workmanship. The cell-work pattern was constructed of small pieces of gold sheet soldered vertically to a gold back-sheet (the effect being like a honeycomb). Every small cell was partially filled with a wax-glue paste, onto which was placed a patterned gold foil, topped by a garnet slice shaped exactly to fit the cell. The garnets were held in place only by the snug fit of the stone in the cell, and in some cases by the slight flattening by burnishing (rubbing with a tool) of the top of the cell walls. The gold foils have very fine grid patterns that reflect light back through the garnets to add sparkle.

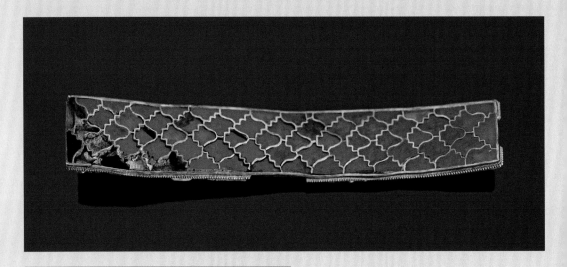

Cloisonné mount and cross-section drawing. The damage at one end reveals the cellular structure and patterned gold foils.
[Photograph: Birmingham Museums Trust; Drawing: C Fern]

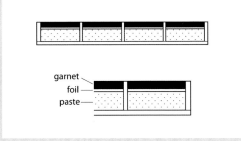

garnet
foil
paste

Every stage of conservation was fully documented using X-radiography (X-ray), photography and written records, information that would complement the research of the objects, their manufacture, form and ornament, wear and damage. The cleaning also revealed fragments and parts that had been completely obscured by soil previously, sometimes contained within the cavities of larger objects, such as with the gold hilt plate **317**. Intriguingly, it was discovered that some cloisonné objects (eg **166**) had cells that didn't contain garnets, but a greenish-white substance that probably represents a decayed inlay but which remains, despite scientific investigation, unidentified.

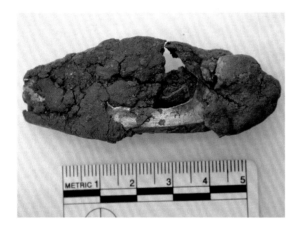

Above: Unidentified inlay on hilt collar **166**.
[Birmingham Museums Trust]

Top left and left: Hilt plate **317** as excavated and
with X-ray showing rivets and other objects
trapped in soil in the interior.
[Photograph: Birmingham Museums Trust; X-ray:
courtesy of Lincolnshire Archives, Lincolnshire
County Council]

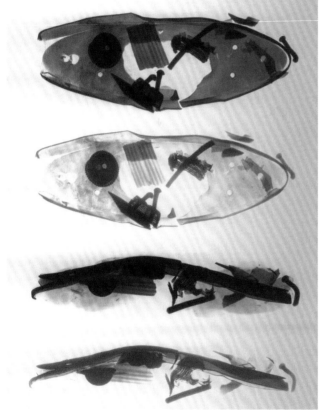

Solving puzzles

The conservation team worked closely with the finds specialist (Chris Fern) throughout the investigative process. As progress was made, it became increasingly clear that the Staffordshire Hoard was like a giant jigsaw puzzle, or rather like many jigsaws, but mixed together with parts missing and no instructions.

Only one item is a complete object, cross pendant **588**; the rest are actually fittings removed from larger 'parent' objects now vanished, such as swords, church equipment and perhaps saddles. These actual objects were not included in the Hoard. For example, there are no sword blades, only the precious-metal parts from their hilts and scabbards.

Gradually, over several years, the fragments were made whole, and the fittings became sets with matching ornament, meaning that ultimately it has been possible to consider what some of the original weapons and other objects looked like.

Sword pyramid **580** was recovered whole, but its pair **581** was reconstructed from several fragments like that shown (not to scale).
[Birmingham Museums Trust]

In Spring 2014, to progress the research process, the entire collection was brought together in the conservation laboratory at Birmingham Museum & Art Gallery for the first time since it was discovered. The finds specialist was given two weeks of intensive study with the objects, and hundreds of relationships were identified or confirmed. Slowly, many of the broken fragments began to be rejoined. Certain rebuilt silver objects proved to be among the more unusual items in the collection (silver, especially, can become brittle when buried, leading to significant fragmentation). They include three large silver pommels (**75–7**) of related form and style that are unparalleled, and also unmatched is a set of silver mounts decorated with niello (**567–71**) reconstructed from more than 70 fragments. Bringing the entire Hoard together also confirmed that there were extensive decorative fittings from at least one helmet, but with no surviving evidence for the iron or leather structure of the cap, one expert compared it to 'trying to rebuild a house when only the wallpaper survives'.

Analysis

Although we might wish to see the Staffordshire Hoard objects in their original, unblemished glory, the damage that is a feature of so many has proved extremely important. As a result, researchers were able to see 'inside' the finds, to examine techniques of construction that are normally hidden, and to take samples for scientific analysis, opportunities not usually possible for complete objects. These investigations have provided new insights into Anglo-Saxon fine metalworking and allowed a better understanding of the Hoard in relation to finds manufactured elsewhere in England and Europe.

Two scientific methods, X-ray fluorescence (XRF) and scanning electron microscopy with energy dispersive X-ray analysis (SEM-EDX), were used to analyse the composition of the metalwork. The gold and silver are not pure but are alloys of several metals, as is typical for the period: for instance, the gold was mixed with small amounts of silver and copper. The gold objects would mostly have been made from melted gold coins imported from mainland Europe, the fineness (the amount of gold relative to other metals) of which varied. Generally, the fineness of the imported coins declined over time, but it appears that the Anglo-Saxon smiths could improve the fineness of objects by adding gold from sources of higher purity, such as coins from the Byzantine Empire. In addition, comparison of the gold alloys of the Hoard objects at the surface level versus the core showed that a process of 'surface enrichment' had been undertaken to remove a small amount of the silver from the gold alloy. This was done by exposing the surface metal to a weak acid, possibly in the form of a paste. This enhanced the metal's outward appearance, for example, by brightening a back-sheet onto which filigree wires were applied.

Niello mounts

Niello is a form of decoration using black inlay. It was formed by placing silver sulphide paste in pre-cut channels on the gold or silver object and heating to 600°C. Set **567–71** comprises five silver mounts with gilt edging and black niello line ornament imitating the geometric patterns seen on cloisonné objects. The set has no direct parallels. The parts are all incomplete, but it has been proposed that they might have decorated a horse bridle, since a large number of rivets were used to attach them, most likely to a flexible material such as leather.

The pair of eye-shaped mounts (possibly decoration for blinkers) can be compared with the eye-shaped mounts in garnet cloisonné (**542–3**). This relationship, and the use of 'mushroom' pattern in the decoration, might mean the set of niello mounts was manufactured in East Anglia.

Niello mount **569** as reconstructed, together with a drawing suggesting how the set of mounts (**567–571**) decorated a horse bridle.
[Photograph: The Potteries Museum & Art Gallery, Stoke-on-Trent; Drawing: C Fern]

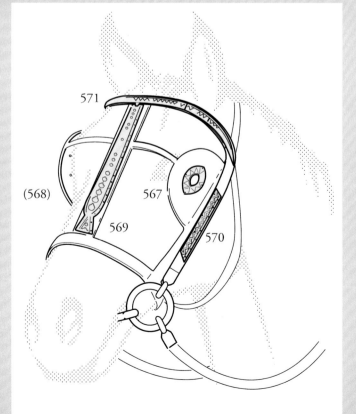

Filigree

The ornate patterns seen on the filigree objects were formed by soldering individual gold (or silver) patterned wires or globules to a metal backsheet. Overall, the tiny scale of the work is extraordinary, with some wires in the Hoard only 0.2mm thick. Mostly, beaded and twisted wires were used in early Anglo-Saxon filigree to form interlace (looping) and zoomorphic (animal-like) patterns, or else herringbone patterns that resemble textile (eg **114–15**). Granules were sometimes used to form the eyes of creatures, but are less common generally. A tool called a beading file was painstakingly used to create the microscopic beaded effect on the wires. So fine is the work that it must have been done in good light, probably in the open air. The parts were most likely fixed in position with a form of organic solder paste that left a near invisible join after heating.

Mount **473** with zoomorphic interlace formed from beaded wires of different thickness. [The Potteries Museum & Art Gallery, Stoke-on-Trent]

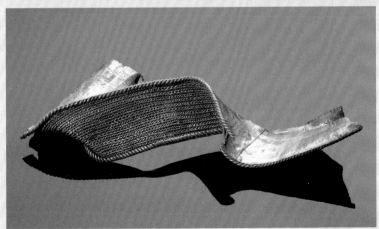

Hilt collar **115** with its textile effect created using rows of twisted wires. [Birmingham Museums Trust]

The compositions of the brilliant red garnets decorating the objects were analysed by a technique known as particle-induced X-ray emission (PIXE) and the results were compared to data for contemporary garnet-decorated objects found elsewhere in Europe established by the *Wellweites Zellwork* (International Framework) project based in Germany. Thanks to this research, dedicated to exploring the origins of the garnets, it has been possible to suggest where the stones employed on the Hoard objects were sourced. Two main types of the mineral were used: pyrope garnets with an origin in the Czech Republic and almandine garnets from India and Sri Lanka. Studies were also conducted on the rarer inlays and other materials found in the Hoard, including glass, wood, bone, pastes and adhesives. Together they have helped illuminate the extensive reach of trade links in the Anglo-Saxon period.

Table of contents of the Staffordshire Hoard.

	Catalogue	Object type	No. objects	Gold
FITTINGS FROM WEAPONRY	1–78	Pommels	74	58
	79–84	Sword rings	3	-
	85–190	Hilt collars	107	97
	191–242	Hilt rings	52	35
	243–409, 696–7	Hilt plates/guards	171	131
	410–526, 533–7	Small mounts (mostly hilt fittings)	122	117
	527–32	Serpent mounts	6	6
	572–84	Pyramid/button fittings	12	10
	585–7	Buckles	3	2
HELMET PARTS	589–92	Crest and cheekpieces		-
	593	Helmet-band with silver sheet inlay		-
	594–604, 606	Die-impressed bands/panels	1	-
	612–13	Reeded strip and clips		-
	615	U-section edging		-
LARGE MOUNTS	538	Bird-fish mount	1	1
	542–66	Cloisonné mounts	25	25
	567–71	Niello mounts	6	-
CHRISTIAN OBJECTS	539	Great cross	1	1
	540	Inscribed strip	1	1
	541	Headdress mount	1	1
	588	Cross pendant	1	1
	607/8	Base with reeded strip	1	-
	676	Locking pins	2	-
FRAGMENTS	609–11	Reeded strip	-	-
	614	U-section edging	-	-
	616–75	Bosses, nails, rivets and washers	-	105
	605, 677–91	Miscellaneous	-	70
	692–5	Loose garnets and foils	-	41
	[K580]	Glass ('eye')	-	-
		Total:	590	702

					Weight by primary material (g)				
Silver	Copper alloy	Garnet	Glass	Stone	Gold	Silver	Copper alloy	Garnet	Stone
16	1 (core)	-	-	-	784.65	254.16	9.59	-	-
3	-	-	-	-	-	30.60	-	-	-
9	1	-	-	-	725.34	75.19	0.84	-	-
16	1	-	-	-	141.55	22.22	0.12	-	-
40	-	-	-	-	591.11	132.23	-	-	-
5	-	-	-	-	248.05	7.64	-	-	-
-	-	-	-	-	70.31	-	-	-	-
2	-	-	-	1	114.62	29.31	-	-	5.30
1	-	-	-	-	7.43	6.06	-	-	-
4	-	-	-	-	48.29	319.82	-	-	-
1 (112 frags)	-	-	-	-	-	55.32	-	-	-
21 (835 frags)	-	-	-	-	-	72.77	-	-	-
3 (677 frags)	-	-	-	-	-	134.95	-	-	-
1 (25 frags)	-	-	-	-	-	29.33	-	-	-
-	-	-	-	-	62.20	-	-	-	-
-	-	-	-	-	750.93	-	-	-	-
6	-	-	-	-	-	158.44	-	-	-
-	-	-	-	-	140.35	-	-	34.90	-
-	-	-	-	-	79.69	-	-	-	-
-	-	-	-	-	70.66	-	-	-	-
-	-	-	-	-	24.38	-	-	-	-
1 (112 frags)	-	-	-	-	-	90.38	-	-	-
2	-	-	-	-	-	1.68	-	-	-
20	-	-	-	-	-	15.69	-	-	-
43	-	-	-	-	-	104.93	-	-	-
157	1	-	-	-	59.81	24.89	0.50	-	-
1132	107	-	-	-	20.24	130.08	5.41	-	-
-	-	74	-	-	0.33	-	-	8.54	-
-	-	-	1	-	-	-	-	-	-
1483	**111**	**74**	**1**	**1**	**3939.94**	**1695.69**	**16.46**	**43.44**	**5.30**

3 What is the Hoard?

Quantity and character

Great treasures capture the imagination, but before the role of the Hoard in the historical events of the 7th century AD can be considered – was it a Mercian royal treasure, did its objects come from a major battle, and why was it buried? – it is first necessary to establish its quantities and character. At the end of conservation and research, almost 4,600 individual fragments and finds had been counted, which after reassembly resulted in a catalogue of 698 entries arranged by object type. Because of the fragmented nature of the collection, with many small nails, rivets and sheet pieces remaining after consolidation, the total number of original objects can only ever be estimated, but approximately 600 are suggested. Across the range of fittings, more than 150 pairs or sets of objects have been matched by form, manufacture or decoration.

Finds specialist Chris Fern working on the collection.
[Birmingham Museums Trust]

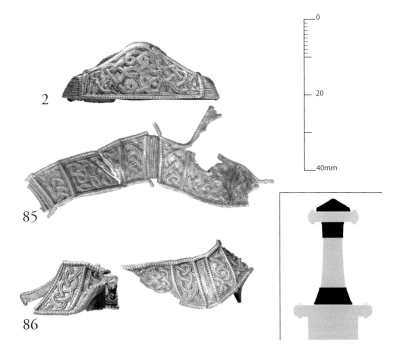

2

85

86

Mass

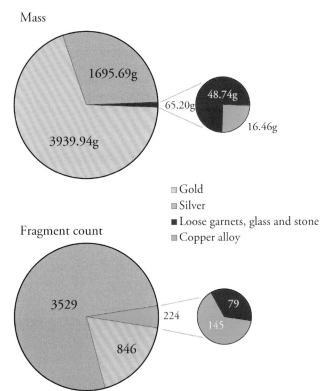

1695.69g

48.74g

65.20g

16.46g

3939.94g

▨ Gold
▨ Silver
■ Loose garnets, glass and stone
▨ Copper alloy

Fragment count

3529

224

79

145

846

Many of the finds are made of more than one material, but, based on the 'primary' metal of each, a total gold weight is indicated of around 4kg. To this is added around 1.7kg of silver, with a very small number of objects and fragments of copper alloy, loose garnets and other small materials. The silver was more fragmented than the gold, and included more than 2,000 pieces of silver and silver-gilt sheet, many of which originated from the highly decorated cap of the helmet.

Within the Hoard are represented almost the full range of art styles and craft techniques seen in fine metalworking of the late 6th to 7th centuries in England. Most of the gold items (401 objects, approximately 60 per cent) feature some form of fine filigree wire or granular ornament, and a smaller number have cloisonné decoration, mainly with garnets (131 objects, approximately 20 per cent). Ornament composed of animal interlace and other bestial motifs,

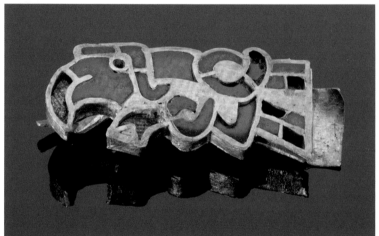

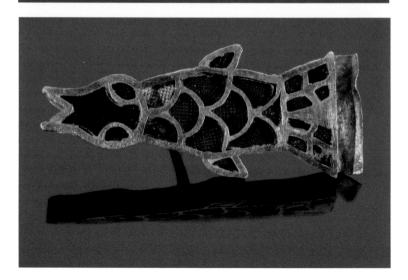

Bird (511–12) and fish (513)
mounts from a weapon hilt in
Salin's Style II (not to scale).
[Birmingham Museums Trust]

mostly of a type known to archaeologists as Salin's Style II (142 objects, approximately 20 per cent), characterises much of the filigree decoration and is also seen on other objects. In addition, some filigree-decorated objects demonstrate a scrollwork style, especially on some fittings from the grips and guards of swords.

The silver pommels and other fittings from weapon hilts were mostly cast, in contrast with the gold items, which were more often made of sheet metal and only rarely cast (eg pommel **57**). Some of the silver objects again have animal ornament. Today the silver has a dulled grey appearance, but traces of gilding (visible or identified by XRF) show that much of it would have appeared gold originally, or been part gilded to achieve a silver and gold bichrome effect. Niello is also present on silver objects and a few in gold (eg **56–7** and **540**), which was used to create further striking contrast.

Pommel **57**, by mass (44g) the greatest of the gold pommels, with unusual sculpted animal art (Style II) and niello line ornament. [The Potteries Museum & Art Gallery, Stoke-on-Trent]

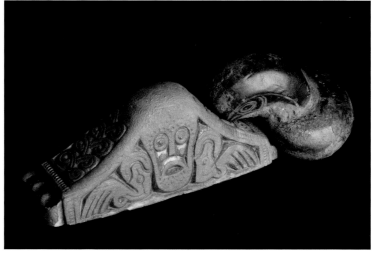

Pommel **68** showing a bearded head between animal legs, together with sword ring **82**. [The Potteries Museum & Art Gallery, Stoke-on-Trent]

Pommel **56** with niello picking out its animal design.
[Birmingham Museums Trust]

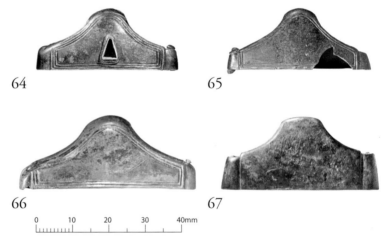

Silver pommels **64–7**.
[Cotswold Archaeology ©
Barbican Research Associates]

A military collection

Around 80 per cent of the objects are decorative fittings from the hilts of bladed weapons or scabbards, and most are probably from swords. The sword typical of the period comprised a long, double-edged iron and steel blade, topped by a spike or tang. The parts making up the hilt, consisting of a hand grip between two guards and a pommel at the end, were attached to the tang. The precious-metal decorations – hilt collars and rings, hilt plates, the pommel cap and small mounts – were applied to the hilt. No blades were included in the Hoard, with only a single small iron fragment of tang remaining inside one gold pommel (**2**). Just two seaxes – fighting knives with a shorter blade and single cutting edge – are definitely evidenced (**55**, **167–9**, **225**, **370**).

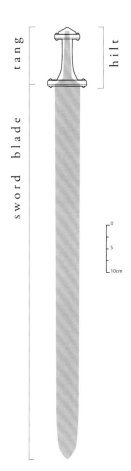

tang

hilt

sword blade

0
5
10cm

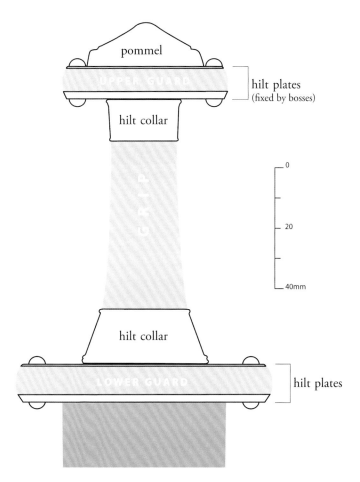

pommel

UPPER GUARD

hilt plates
(fixed by bosses)

hilt collar

TANG

0

20

40mm

hilt collar

LOWER GUARD

hilt plates

The typical sword and hilt of the period.
[C Fern]

Gold hilt plate **370** from a seax.
[The Potteries Museum & Art Gallery, Stoke-on-Trent]

Gold, garnet and glass cloisonné fittings (**55, 167–9, 225**) from the hilt of a seax, a 'princely' weapon.
[The Potteries Museum & Art Gallery, Stoke-on-Trent]

Construction of a sword hilt

An almost complete set of gold fittings from a sword hilt was found at Market Rasen (Lincolnshire) in 1997. The discovery was made by a metal detectorist and the nature of the original deposit is uncertain: possibly it represents a sword placed or lost in a river that was nearby, later disturbed by dredging. The parts are close parallels for the Hoard's sets of pommel caps and hilt collars in gold filigree, and for the hilt plates from guards (originally the sword probably had four plates, only two of which remain). Analysis at the British Museum of mineral-preserved organic remains within the collars has shown the sword grip was of oak (*Quercus* sp) and the guards of blackthorn or related wood (*Prunus* sp).

Hilt fittings from Market Rasen.
[Trustees of the British Museum]

Overall, remains survive of a minimum of 74 pommel caps; 130 hilt collars and hilt rings from grips; three silver sword rings for attachment to pommels; and around 122 small mounts of other forms from weapon grips and guards. It is difficult to ascertain the original number of hilt plates from guards represented, as some are very fragmented, but perhaps as many as 170. As it is possible, or even likely, that some of the mounts could have come from sword hilts without metal pommels, or with iron pommels formed with the tang, the number of pommels probably does not equate with the maximum number of swords and seaxes represented. Nonetheless, at a conservative estimate, probably in excess of 100 weapons were stripped to produce the Hoard assemblage. A relative proportion of 4:1 gold to silver finds indicates that weapons with silver hilt fittings were in the minority.

In addition, there are five pairs of pyramid fittings (**572–81**) and a single pair of button fittings (**582–4**) from scabbards (a single stone bead fits one of the buttons), as well as three small buckles (**585–7**) that

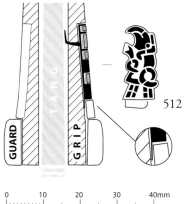

512

How mounts **511–13** were recessed into the grip (see p 24). [C Fern]

Pair of pyramid fittings **578–9** and buttons **582–4** (buttons not to scale). [Cotswold Archaeology © Barbican Research Associates, The Potteries Museum & Art Gallery, Stoke-on-Trent]

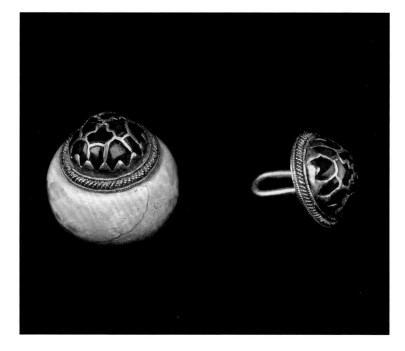

Two gold and one silver (**585–7**) buckle from the Hoard. [Cotswold Archaeology © Barbican Research Associates]

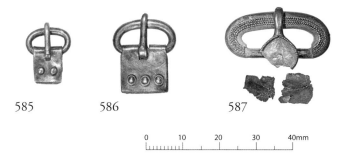

585   586   587

might be from weapon harness. The only definite armour is the helmet, from which a crest (**589–90**) and pair of cheekpieces survive (**591–2**), along with large but heavily fragmented quantities of silver-gilt sheet and other fixings (**593–7, 599–604, 606, 611–13** and **673**) that would have decorated its missing iron and leather cap.

There are a number of large and highly impressive mounts that are not interpreted as from weaponry. One of gold sheet (**538**) has an alloy of high purity and a resulting beautiful buttery gold colour, showing a fish held by birds of prey. Twenty-five large mounts that form six sets (**542–66**) have matching, high-quality garnet cloisonné, their closely related manufacture suggesting production in a single workshop, as with the set of silver and niello mounts (**567–71**) that share aspects of form and style with them. All are without ready parallels, so it is difficult to be sure what they decorated, beyond the fact that all must represent commissions for recipients or institutions of the highest order. The use of some for the ornamentation of elite equestrian equipment is possible, such as saddles and horse harness.

Great gold cross **539** with garnet settings, folded as found. [Birmingham Museums Trust]

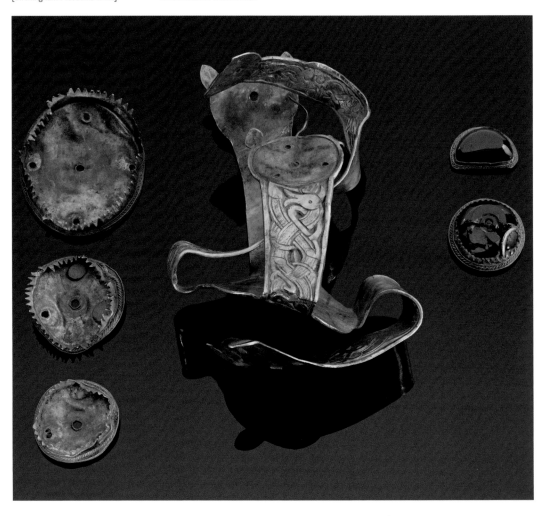

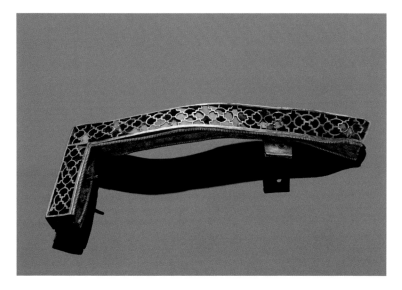

Possible book mount **562**, one of
a set of three in gold and garnet
cloisonné.
[Birmingham Museums Trust]

Christian equipment

A small group of objects of certain Christian function are some of the
largest and most significant artefacts in the Hoard. A great gold cross
(**539**) is decorated with animal art and was originally studded with large
cabochon garnets. After dismantling, its loose settings were parcelled in
its folded arms, and altogether its parts make it the heaviest item (175g)
in the collection. A gold strip (**540**) bent in half is inscribed with a Latin
biblical text, one of the earliest examples yet found. It invokes a warlike
prayer for God's wrath upon enemies, and might represent the arm of a
second large cross. In addition, some of the large cloisonné-decorated
mounts might have come from sacred objects, such as a gospel-book cover
(**562–4**) or reliquary (**542–7**), a container for sacred objects.

Several items may have been worn to indicate Christian belief, such
as small crosses (**481–2**), which might have adorned clothing or war gear.
The gold cross pendant (**588**) with filigree ornament may have been worn
by a significant ecclesiastical figure of the early Christian Church, such
as a priest or bishop. Finally, a unique mount (**541**) is formed of a low-
conical disc, with garnet cloisonné and animal art, on which is mounted
a second smaller disc topped by a chequered glass millefiori stud. Dubbed
the 'mystery object' by museum staff at first, it was probably part of an
ecclesiastical headdress.

Selection

The Staffordshire Hoard is a select assemblage, therefore, composed
chiefly of precious-metal fittings dismantled from the hilts of swords,
but together with other unusual and significant prestige objects.
Besides the absence of the iron weapon blades, the organic and
other non-valuable parts were also mostly excluded. The Hoard is,
furthermore, 'incomplete' in other interesting and important ways,

Gold and garnet pendant from
Hammerwich.
[The Potteries Museum & Art
Gallery, Stoke-on-Trent]

at least in terms of what we might consider ought to be in a treasure of the 7th century. The Potteries Museum & Art Gallery (Stoke-on-Trent) holds one small garnet pendant found not far from the Hoard, also in Hammerwich parish, which would once have been part of the costume of an elite Anglo-Saxon woman. Feminine jewellery, such as pendants and brooches, is a find category completely missing from the Hoard, yet such accessories occur typically in high-status female graves of the period. Rather, as shown, the collection has an overtly martial character, though even so some objects associated with the warrior elite known from other sites are also largely absent, such as ornate belt-buckles and feasting gear. Lastly, no coins were included, although these were still novel in early 7th-century England and especially so in the borderlands of Mercia.

It is possible to see everything in the collection as originating from the battlefield: the weapons, helmet and saddle parts, as well as the Christian objects, carried to war perhaps as talismans of the new religion. However, only the weaponry and equipment of a commanding elite are represented; entirely missing are the iron fittings from spears and shields of the rank and file on the battlefield. In terms of the swords, too, the weapons of the Hoard are quite different from most examples found in contemporary 'warrior' graves known from the archaeological record, which are either without metal hilt fittings or which have less prestigious fittings of copper-alloy metal. Although such plainer swords were still of high value, they do not proclaim the same top tier of status. In sum, the Hoard stands as a record of the prestige gear of warrior leaders, princes and even kings, of a small number of high-ranking churchmen and possibly bishops, but it tells us nothing of the ordinary soldier class, and so its value is partial as a source for telling us about the make-up of an army of the period.

Other high-status metalwork known from the 7th century has come from cemeteries, princely graves and, increasingly, as single finds discovered by metal detectorists, but other hoards of precious metal are very rare in Britain at this period. Examples of rich graves with comparable material culture include those at Sutton Hoo (Suffolk), Taplow (Buckinghamshire) and Prittlewell (Essex). These graves and the finds in them have detailed archaeological information to help with their understanding; however, the two best parallels for the Hoard's gold filigree art styles – the hilt fittings from Market Rasen and Cumberland – are by contrast poorly understood discoveries. It is not known how these finds originally entered the archaeological record, or even exactly where they were found, which undermines confidence in attaching the styles they represent to any particular archaeological or historical setting.

A find without parallel

The fact that so few hoards are known from early Anglo-Saxon England makes the find from Staffordshire all the more astonishing. A hoard can be defined as a collection of items of value, deliberately buried, though there might be different reasons why this was done. If the burial was for safe-keeping, with the intention of recovery, then the motivation was economic and protective, but with some ill fate suffered by the depositor leading to the cache's loss; or if the intention was 'ritual', then the treasure might deliberately have been put out of circulation, as a gift for a god, for example, never to be reclaimed. Each of these cases is different from the more typical way that precious objects were deposited in the early Anglo-Saxon period, that is as grave goods for the dead.

Sites at Crondall (Hampshire) and most recently 'near Swaffham' (Norfolk) have produced small coin assemblages of contemporary date to the Hoard, but in character they are very different. Gold coinage production started in some Anglo-Saxon kingdoms as early as the late 6th century, but relatively few of these first coins circulated as far as Mercia, which was among the last of the Anglo-Saxon territories to take up coin minting. It is not until the 9th century and the Viking period that the practice of hoarding precious metal became more frequent in the British Isles. In Europe, more examples of coin and precious-metal hoards have been found, though again none is directly comparable. One of the largest was discovered in 1774 at Tureholm (Sweden), containing 12kg of gold objects of the 5th and 6th centuries AD. But very little now survives of the original find (most was melted down), and although it includes some weapon fittings, it is not exclusively of martial character. More common in Scandinavia in the same period were small ritual or votive offerings, often made in the ground, of gold pendants called bracteates. With only a few exceptions, such practice does not seem to have been adopted in England, unless it is the case that some of the single finds made by metal detectorists, of precious-metal objects including pommels and other hilt fittings (eg Market Rasen), could in fact be votive in intent, rather than simple, accidental losses.

The battlefield character of the collection invites comparison with a succession of mass deposits of weaponry made at wetland sites in south Scandinavia and north Germany, such as Nydam (Denmark) and Thorsberg (Germany). However, there are important differences, not least that these deposits are typically earlier in date and had ended by the 6th century AD. Moreover, whereas the Hoard represents a select collection representing only material culture from the warrior elite, at the northern European sites the full equipment of defeated armies is present, ceremonially destroyed – spears, shields, swords, and other gear – from the rank and file through to mounted commanders.

Accounts of hoards and treasure also occur in the literary and historical record. The Anglo-Saxon epic poem *Beowulf* does not celebrate the avaricious act of hoarding but rather praises acts of generous giving by kings to warrior followers. Near the end of the poem, the hero Beowulf is killed fighting a dragon. Some of its mighty golden treasure is given out as rewards, but the rest is reburied, its unbearable cost requiring that it be forsaken: 'they let the ground keep that ancestral treasure, gold under gravel, gone to earth, as useless to men now as it ever was' (Heaney 2000, lines 3163–8). In another episode is described the looting of weapons and armour from the slain on the battlefield: 'they were left masters of the blood-soaked battleground. One warrior stripped the other, looted Ongentheow's iron mail-coat, his hard sword-hilt, his helmet too' (Heaney 2000, lines 2985–7).

Anglo-Saxon and British historical sources further record treasure giving and taking. Valuable items or coinage could be given as tribute to aggressors to avoid war, a tactic of paying off enemies. One example around the time of the Hoard is the royal treasure of 'greater gifts than can be imagined', according to Bede (HE III, 24), which was offered in AD 655 to Penda by King Oswiu of Northumbria in an attempt to get the Mercian ruler to stop savaging the northern kingdom. Another strategy of Anglo-Saxon kingdoms was to take valuable loot, cattle and slaves by raiding. In the Welsh poem 'Marwnad Cynddylan' ('The Death Song of Cynddylan') an attack by warriors from Powys into Mercia resulted in 'extensive spoils' taken from Lichfield, an event that was probably close to

Beowulf

The epic poem *Beowulf* is one of the earliest great works of English literature. The surviving version was probably written down in the 8th or 9th century, but the fictional events and culture described may have drawn on earlier oral tradition of the 5th to 7th centuries. Composed possibly in East Anglia, though set in Scandinavia, it follows the adventures of the warrior Beowulf as he comes to the assistance of the Danish King Hrothgar, first by killing the warrior-devouring Grendel and then Grendel's monstrous mother. Beowulf is richly rewarded, then returns home to become king of the Geats, where years later he is obliged to fight a treasure-hoarding dragon. In the ensuing battle he is slain, his body is cremated, and his grave marked with a barrow. The poem's themes of warrior life, weaponry and treasure provide an evocative context for the Staffordshire Hoard objects.

the time of the collection and burial of the Staffordshire Hoard (Rowlands 1990, 174–89).

Lamentably, as much as we would wish it, it is not possible to link any historical incident directly with the Hoard. Our sources are too few, there must have been innumerable other happenings of which we have no record, and we cannot date the treasure accurately enough. However, such accounts do provide intriguing models of how such a quantity of precious metalwork could have come together in the political context of the frequent raiding and warfare that characterised the formation of the Mercian kingdom during the 7th century.

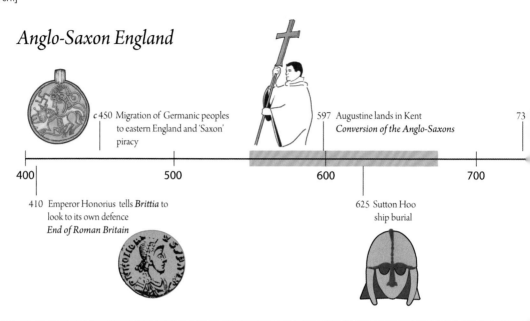

Anglo-Saxon England

c 450 Migration of Germanic peoples
to eastern England and 'Saxon'
piracy

597 Augustine lands in Kent
Conversion of the Anglo-Saxons

73

400   500   600   700

410 Emperor Honorius tells *Brittia* to
look to its own defence
End of Roman Britain

625 Sutton Hoo
ship burial

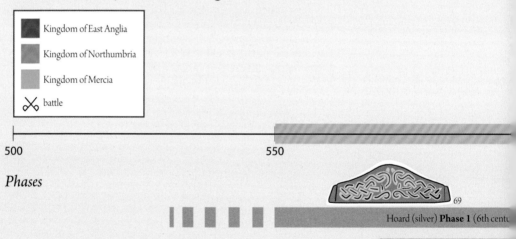

Date-range of the Staffordshire Hoard's metalwork phases and art, with key historical reigns and battles

- ■ Kingdom of East Anglia
- ■ Kingdom of Northumbria
- ■ Kingdom of Mercia
- ✗ battle

500   550

Phases

69

Hoard (silver) **Phase 1** (6th centu

Hoard (gold) **Phase 2** (*c* 570–*c* 6

Art

Style I

182

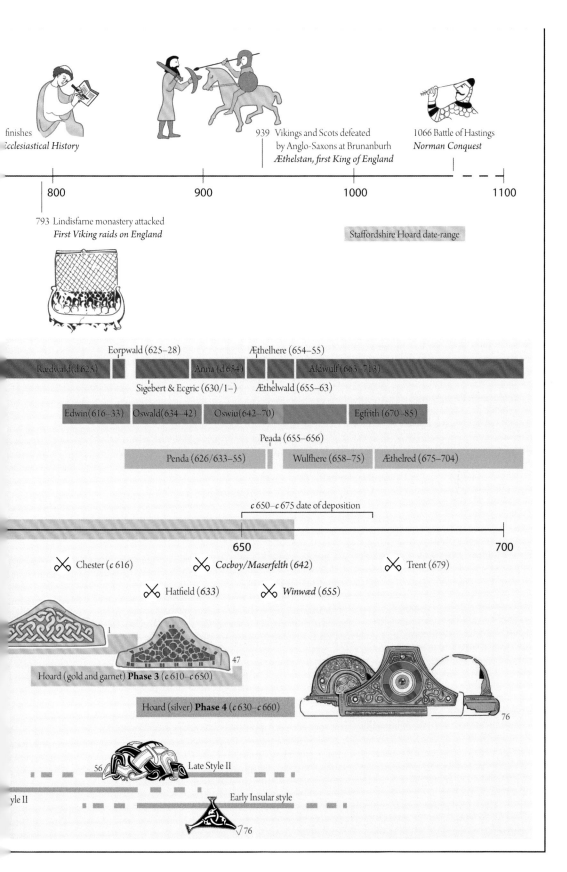

finishes
Ecclesiastical History

939 Vikings and Scots defeated
by Anglo-Saxons at Brunanburh
Æthelstan, first King of England

1066 Battle of Hastings
Norman Conquest

| 800 | 900 | 1000 | 1100 |

793 Lindisfarne monastery attacked
First Viking raids on England

Staffordshire Hoard date-range

Eorpwald (625–28)   Æthelhere (654–55)

Rædwald (d 625)   Anna (d 654)   Aldwulf (663–713)

Sigebert & Ecgric (630/1–)   Æthelwald (655–63)

Edwin (616–33)   Oswald (634–42)   Oswiu (642–70)   Egfrith (670–85)

Peada (655–656)

Penda (626/633–55)   Wulfhere (658–75)   Æthelred (675–704)

c 650–*c* 675 date of deposition

| 650 | 700 |

⚔ Chester (*c* 616)   ⚔ *Cocboy/Maserfelth* (642)   ⚔ Trent (679)

⚔ Hatfield (633)   ⚔ *Winwæd* (655)

Hoard (gold and garnet) **Phase 3** (*c* 610–*c* 650)

Hoard (silver) **Phase 4** (*c* 630–*c* 660)

Late Style II

yle II

Early Insular style

4 Jewel of Mercia

Dating the Hoard

The Hoard is difficult to date with the accuracy we would desire. In archaeology, 'absolute' dates are provided when material can be securely associated with dateable objects like coins (linked with historical reigns of kings or moneyers) or by scientific means, most commonly by radiocarbon analysis of organic remains. However, the collection contains no coins and its very limited organics were not available for scientific dating at the time of the project. Instead, 'relative' dating was employed, which is based on consideration of object forms and art styles in relation to dated material from elsewhere in Britain and Europe. Ultimately, establishing when the Hoard was deposited in the ground depends on determining the date of the latest find (or group of objects) within it. However, there is also the 'heirloom' factor, as objects might be in use for many years after manufacture, skewing the dating by decades. Therefore, the degree of wear on objects must also be taken into account.

Examination of the Hoard metalwork has concluded that the collection was most likely deposited between *c* AD 650 and *c* 675. The objects were manufactured over a considerable period before that, however, with about a century separating the earliest and latest. Furthermore, based on the styles of the objects, it seems highly likely that the metalwork originated from more than one region. In all, four groups or phases of metalwork have been suggested.

The oldest objects are a small number of silver weapon fittings, dating from as early as the mid-6th century to the early 7th century AD, some of which can be considered to have come from 'heirloom' swords. Examples include pommel **68** and pair of hilt collars **182–3**. The majority of the collection's objects fall into two groups, however: earlier gold objects, characteristically hilt fittings with filigree ornament, produced *c* AD 570–*c* 630; and later gold objects of *c* AD 610–*c* 650, including the church objects and the majority of the large cloisonné mounts. Latest is a small but important group of silver weapon fittings that have gold mounts and which exhibit a distinctive 'Early Insular style' of ornament, dating from *c* AD 630–*c* 660.

It is believed that these groups reflect, to an extent, changes in the availability of gold over time. The bulk of the gold objects represent a period from the late 6th to mid-7th centuries when the precious metal became suddenly but only briefly more abundant in the metal economy, whereas the early and late silver phases of metalwork reflect the opposite: periods of gold poverty preceding and succeeding this 'golden age'.

Silver pommel **68** was very likely made in Scandinavia, but all the rest of the objects are Anglo-Saxon. The question of where exactly they were made is fundamental to understanding the significance of the Hoard and the role it might have played in the turbulent history of 7th-century

Mercia and England. There have been few comparable finds of high-status metalwork from the wider landscape of the Hoard to support a case for manufacture by Mercian craftsmen, whereas similar metalwork is associated in particular with Anglo-Saxon kingdoms in the south-east, such as East Anglia and Kent. Indeed, the different ornamental styles of the metalwork allow for the possibility that the objects came from different workshops producing equipment in regionally distinctive 'kingdom styles' for leading warriors and rulers.

Mercia

The Mierce were the 'people of the border', since what is now the Midlands region was where Anglo-Saxon culture merged with British (Welsh) culture in the west. Mercia would become a great kingdom, but at c AD 600 it probably comprised a patchwork of small 'folk' territories, still to be unified. It was in the reign of Penda (c AD 626/33–655) and the time of the Staffordshire Hoard that its establishment truly began, forged perhaps by a need for military cooperation in the face of raiding from the already powerful kingdoms of Northumbria and East Anglia.

That local groups retained some autonomy within the early kingdom is nevertheless suggested by Bede's statement that the River Trent separated the north Mercians from the south Mercians (HE III, 24). By the early 8th century, the kingdom comprised a total of 12,000 hides, a hide being the measure of land needed to support one farmstead and household. The heart of Mercia may have lain in the lands around the River Tame (south of Lichfield) and Roman Watling Street. This was the territory of the Tomsæte tribe from which Penda's dynasty might have originated. A palace was later sited locally at Tamworth, while a bishopric was founded at Lichfield in AD 669 by St Chad.

Mercia's power reached its peak in the reign of King Offa (d AD 796) around one hundred years after the Hoard. This period saw the kingdom exercise wide and long-lasting influence throughout southern England. During this time, the great boundary with Wales known as Offa's Dyke was constructed, and there was flowering achievement in manuscript art, sculpture and metalworking. However, Mercian power in the following century was increasingly tested by the kingdom of Wessex, and further suffered from Viking incursions and settlement. By the 11th century, the earls of Mercia were influential but subordinate to the nobility of Wessex, a power that ended with King Harold's defeat at Hastings.

Development of kingdoms

The historical and archaeological sources for the 5th to 7th centuries present a period of great change and complexity in what is known across Europe as the 'Migration Period'. It is not surprising that scholars disagree, therefore, about exactly what happened at the end of 'Roman Britain' and about what form 'Anglo-Saxon England' took in this early period. The traditional model saw Germanic groups from north-western Europe, in particular the Angles, Saxons and Jutes, migrating to Britain in the 5th century, bringing with them what became known as Anglo-

Saxon culture. They created kingdoms which spread west, dominating surviving Romano-British communities through conquest and warfare. However, recent scholarship has suggested greater continuity from the Roman period, especially in agricultural land use and the organisation of regional groups. Undoubtedly, considerable change can be seen in the archaeological record, such as a shift from building in stone to timber, a wholesale change in brooch and other costume fashions, and the introduction of new ceramic traditions, all of which are best paralleled in north-western Europe. In addition, the language of Old English, closely related to the tongues of the north Continent, came to dominate. But the degree to which these changes were generated by large- or even small-scale movement of peoples, or by the adoption of new styles and ideas by existing elite groups, is far from clear.

Certainly, at the time when the metalwork of the Hoard was in use (c AD 550–660), the nature of both regional rule and religious belief was in transformation. Regional kingdoms named in historical sources and characterised by associated styles of material culture were emerging. One example is the kingdom of Kent, where workshops producing distinctive disc-brooch fashions for the ruling elite were operating from the mid-6th century. Control over land and resources, as well as military recruitment, depended ultimately on the support of local warrior leaders, whose service was rewarded with treasure or marriage alliances. The pursuit of ever greater economic resources resulted in an almost permanent state of warfare between the emerging realms. But the kingdoms of Anglo-Saxon England did not emerge simultaneously or equal in power. The kingdom of Kent was one of the earliest royal territories to enjoy a period of regional dominance, and East Anglia and Northumbria had become similarly powerful by the early 7th century. All doubtless benefited in their development from trade and contact with foreign kingdoms located around the North Sea. In contrast, the kingdom of Mercia was late to develop, perhaps because in its largely landlocked border location it had less access to the wealth created by overseas trade.

Bede acknowledged Penda of Mercia as the supreme military commander of his age. His conquests saw the territory rise from obscurity to dominance by the time of his death in AD 655 at the Battle of Winwæd. This defeat after such a long period of rule must have brought crisis to the border kingdom and its dynasty, and it was followed just a year later by the murder of Penda's successor and son, Peada. Nevertheless, another period of Mercian supremacy was returned under Wulfhere (AD 658–75).

Mercia in the 7th century

The Hoard findspot sits roughly between two 'folk' groups within Mercia, the Pencersæte and Tomsæte, known from historical sources. The immediate surrounding area has produced little archaeological evidence for early Anglo-Saxon settlement, with the suggestion made that the local landscape was marginal, unimproved land, possibly thinly wooded. The most significant feature is the Roman road of Watling Street that runs

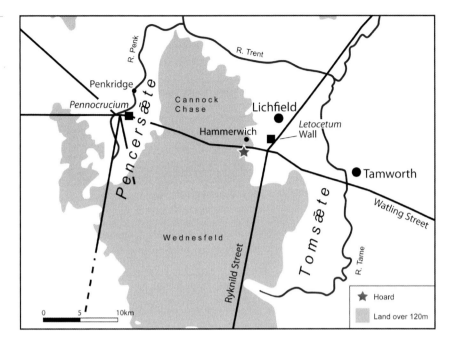

The Hoard find site and its local context.
[C Fern]

beside the site, which would have remained a major route in the period, leading from the east into Mercia. Further north, the River Trent formed another arterial connection, leading to the Humber Estuary in the north-east and ultimately to the sea.

Excavation close to the Trent, at Catholme (Staffordshire), about 10 miles from the Hoard findspot, has revealed a settlement occupied for several hundred years, its buildings and livestock enclosures shifting in their location on the site as they were periodically rebuilt and renewed. It is possible, though not certain, that a nearby Anglo-Saxon cemetery at Wychnor was associated with the earliest phase of occupation at Catholme, with finds of brooches and weapon parts in graves indicating Anglo-Saxon occupation or adopted culture in the region prior to *c* AD 550.

A Mercian social elite is less conspicuous in archaeological terms than in other regions, but is marked by some examples. Rich warrior graves at Barlaston (Staffordshire) and Benty Grange (Derbyshire) of the 7th century included bronze hanging bowls, luxury imports from the west or north of the British Isles, and the latter also contained a helmet formed of bands of iron, topped by a boar figurine and with a silver cross on the nasal, marking a Christian. Occasional single finds of high-status metalwork have also come from the region, including a gold and garnet pommel from Maxstoke Priory (Warwickshire), a highly unusual gold brooch from near Lichfield, and the Hammerwich pendant, although there is no certainty such objects were made close to where they were found. In addition, cropmarks have revealed large timber hall complexes at sites within the region, including at Hatton Rock (Warwickshire) and Frogmore (Shropshire).

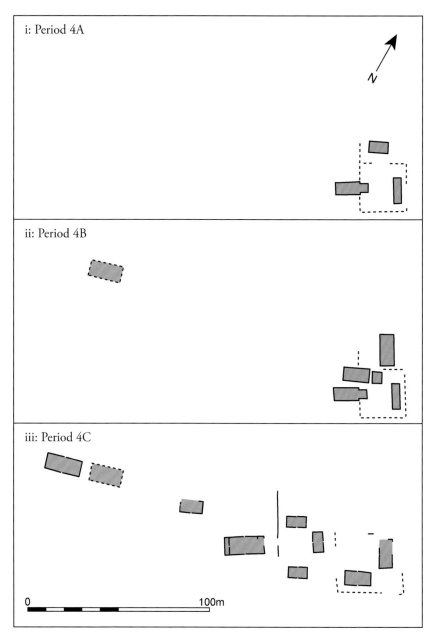

i: Period 4A

ii: Period 4B

iii: Period 4C

0   100m

Settlement phases showing hall
buildings at Catholme (after
Hines).
[C Fern]

Loom weight from Catholme.
[The Potteries Museum & Art Gallery, Stoke-on-Trent]

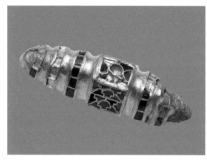

Gold brooch from Streethay,
Lichfield, and pommel from
Maxstoke Priory (Warwickshire).
[Potteries Museum & Art Gallery]

0   10   20   30   40mm

Large hall showing as rectangular
cropmarks on aerial photograph at
Frogmore (Shropshire).
[© CPAT 89-C-0252]

Mercia's neighbours

The Hoard is a treasure out of place. If it could have been predicted
where such a remarkable discovery might have been made, most experts
would probably have placed it in south-east England, perhaps within
the kingdoms of Kent or East Anglia – where the majority of comparable
high-status metalwork has been found – or else within the powerful
northern kingdom of Northumbria. Cemeteries overflowing with locally
made elite metalwork and luxury imports, like at Faversham or Kingston
Down (Kent) and at Sutton Hoo (Suffolk), indicate the existence of stable
rulership by the later 6th to early 7th centuries, commanding productive
farming economies, trade focused on newly established port sites, and
specialist manufacture capable of flawless regalia.

   This power can be linked with the establishment of royal dynasties
recorded in the historical record. Æthelberht of Kent (c AD 590–616) was,
according to the history of Bede, one of a small number of Anglo-Saxon
kings to have exercised widespread power over other kingdoms, and this
overlord status was subsequently succeeded to by Rædwald of East Anglia
and then by rulers of Northumbria. Archaeological investigation of royal
residences and settlements at Lyminge (Kent), Rendlesham (Suffolk) and

Yeavering (Northumberland) have identified large timber hall complexes, as well as evidence of workshops and trade, showing they were important 'central places' within their kingdoms, vital as seats of power, and as administrative and economic hubs. With the arrival of Christianity around c AD 600, monasteries and churches were rapidly founded, becoming new symbols of power, sometimes linked to existing high-status settlements. Thus, at Lyminge a double monastery complex under royal patronage was established alongside the secular settlement.

Little in the archaeological or historical record suggests Mercia was as developed as its neighbours in this period, and yet the great Staffordshire treasure found its way there to be buried within the kingdom in the middle of the 7th century.

Plated disc-brooch from Kingston Down (Kent).
[National Museums Liverpool (World Museum)]

Integrated complex of timber structures under excavation at Lyminge (Kent).
[Department of Archaeology, University of Reading]

5 Weapons and warfare

Famous weapons, leading warriors

Above all, the Staffordshire Hoard's many objects speak of the upper warrior class that supported and enabled royal power in the Anglo-Saxon kingdoms. The ornate-hilted swords and other prestige war gear were the currency of that power: made in royal workshops, such objects were gifted by kings to leading warriors to seal a bond of loyalty. Thanks to the Hoard, that warrior culture now appears much richer than previously thought – gold bedecked – and it is possible also that the owners of the gold-hilted swords were actual participants in the warfare and kingdom-building described in Bede's *Ecclesiastical History* and other sources.

But in the society of the day, great weapons could be important beyond their function and material value. In the poem *Beowulf*, several famous swords are described, including the named Hrunting and Nægling. As heirloom weapons of repute, they illustrate that the sword was not only *the* instrument and symbol of political power in the period, but that individual blades might even be personified and take on legendary status by virtue of success in battle.

That early Anglo-Saxon society was a warrior society is shown by the incidence of weapon symbolism in cemeteries of the 5th to 7th centuries. Around 10–30 per cent of burials typically contain weapons, indicating

Suite of matching sword fittings (**47** and **159–60**) decorated with mushroom-shaped garnets. [Cotswold Archaeology © Barbican Research Associates]

the deceased of a ruling warrior class. However, only a minority of graves include swords alongside more common spear and shield remains, hence sword graves are considered to indicate individuals of higher status. Yet the vast bulk of known swords are not the match of those attested by the fittings of the Hoard, or those from Sutton Hoo Mound 1, Market Rasen and Cumberland. Perhaps it is the case that such prestige weapons were more likely to acquire famous reputations, and so were only very rarely buried. Nevertheless, there are some instances of swords from graves that show modifications or fittings added over time, providing further evidence of ancestral weapons that were kept long in circulation.

Cutting-edge technology

Anglo-Saxon swords were heavy slashing weapons up to 1m in length that, with or without gold fittings, had expertly crafted and prized blades made by a smithing technique known as pattern welding. The method forged together twisted rods of low-carbon iron to form a core to a flat blade, to which steel cutting edges were added. This created a strong yet flexible blade that would take a sharp edge, and with a complex pattern

Replica pattern-welded sword blade.
[Paul Mortimer]

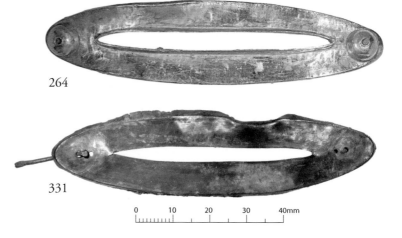

264

331

Hilt plates **264** and **331** from the lower guard showing the slots for the double-edged blades.
[Cotswold Archaeology ©
Barbican Research Associates]

0   10   20   30   40mm

resulting along the length from etching or polishing of the flattened rods. Blade width was around 50–60mm, with the parallel or slightly tapered edges running to a point. The sword fittings in the Hoard would mostly have been fitted to blades of this type, and the shape of those blades can be seen preserved in the slots of some of the lower hilt plates.

Seax fighting knives varied in length and had only a single cutting edge. The weapon would have been relied upon when the press of battle prevented the wielding of a long sword. The reconstruction of the Hoard seax with gold and garnet fittings (**55**, **167–9** and **225**) is based on an example from Gotland, since the Swedish island has produced most parallels for the form of the hilt parts.

The sword hilt of the period was typically of tripartite form (of three parts) and crafted from organic materials, including horn, wood or bone, the grip being set between a pair of upper and lower guards, which were decorated with hilt plates. This arrangement was usually secured at the end of the tang by a pommel that was attached to the upper guard with rivets. As well as being functional, the pommel could of course be of precious metal and highly ornate. The 74 examples in the collection vary in size from 30mm to 60mm in length, with pommel **57** being the largest, as well as the heaviest in gold weight (44g), with bold animal ornament to match.

The collection's many hilt-plate parts suggest some weapons stripped to form the collection had full sets of four plates, with two decorating each guard. Other weapons probably had only two, or even just a single plate on the underside of the lower guard surrounding the junction of hilt and blade. The majority of the plates are of thin gold sheet, with bosses at the ends that covered rivets. In some cases the bosses take the form of small set cabochon garnets. A smaller number of plates are cast silver, and there is also a highly unusual pair of actual silver guards (**409**) that were decorated with gold mounts. Few of the gold plates have ornament beyond garnet bosses, but an outstanding exception is seax plate **370** with a cast animal design.

Reconstruction of seax **55, 167–9** and **225** (see p 27). Analysis has shown the pommel has a different gold composition to the rest of the fittings, so it is possible it was added later as a repair.
[C Fern]

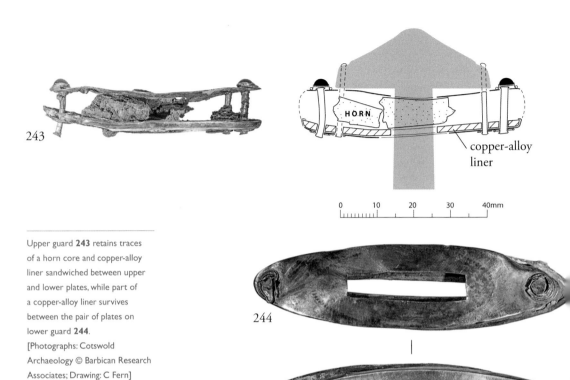

243

HORN

copper-alloy
liner

0   10   20   30   40mm

Upper guard **243** retains traces of a horn core and copper-alloy liner sandwiched between upper and lower plates, while part of a copper-alloy liner survives between the pair of plates on lower guard **244**.
[Photographs: Cotswold Archaeology © Barbican Research Associates; Drawing: C Fern]

244

Mounts **499–502** retain the shape of the guards they were fitted to, with one pair smaller than the other.
[Cotswold Archaeology © Barbican Research Associates]

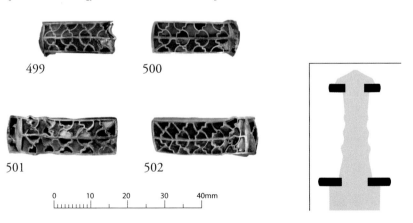

499

500

501

502

0   10   20   30   40mm

Pair of hilt collars **97–8** preserving the oval profile of the grip (not to scale). [Birmingham Museums Trust]

Mounts **439–42**, which would have decorated the grip or guards. [Cotswold Archaeology © Barbican Research Associates]

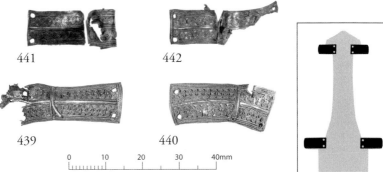

441

442

439

440

0 10 20 30 40mm

More than 50 pairs of collars or rings from the top and bottom of the grip are suggested, and some have been matched with pommels. This shows that weapons were clearly produced with suites of fittings in distinctive filigree and cloisonné styles. Another style of hilt furniture is indicated by the small mounts of varying form (eg **439–42**). Also with a high incidence of sets, they are related to those on the Cumberland hilt. The mounts would have been recessed into the grip and guards so they were flush and were fixed with small nails and probably an adhesive.

Many of the fittings show signs of wear, in the most extreme cases having resulted in the complete flattening of areas of raised ornament or in the perforation of the original metal. Examining the degree of wear on each object provides information about its age when deposited.

Examples of wear on pommels **2** and **68**.
[Birmingham Museums Trust; The Potteries Museum & Art Gallery, Stoke-on-Trent]

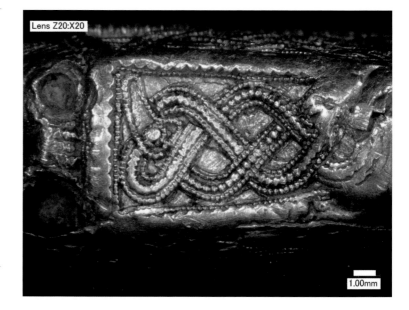

Schematic showing main locations of wear (red lines) on the hilt fittings. The blue line shows the location of polishing marks.
[C Fern]

Hilt collar **157**. The amber replacement for a missing garnet (far left) has decayed during burial (not to scale).
[Birmingham Museums Trust]

1.00mm

In addition, patterns identified have allowed consideration of how the wear occurred. This suggests that the ornate swords were routinely worn in a scabbard at the waist as part of elite warrior costume, with abrasion occurring as a result of the hilt rubbing against clothing. The tops and ends of pommels often showed most damage, which might have been exacerbated by the habit of resting a hand on the hilt of the scabbarded sword. In contrast, there is no obvious damage from use in combat, although there are a number of instances of repair. Pommel **49** had two of its garnets replaced with red glass, and hilt collar **157** has an amber setting in place of a lost stone.

There are also polishing marks on hilt plates, in the form of fine parallel scratches on the underside plates of the lower guard, where the hilt joins the blade. It is believed the scratches on these fittings resulted from the maintenance of the iron blades, which would have required frequent burnishing to prevent rusting, as well as to best display their pattern-welded designs. A will of the late Anglo-Saxon period records the existence of a specialist servant known as a 'sword-polisher', and it is possible such individuals existed earlier.

'I go forth in mail-shirt and shield'

Some of the silver-gilt panels (**596–7**) that had decorated the helmet depict heavily armed marching warriors wearing helmets and mail shirts, with swords at the waist, and carrying spears and shields. They represent the idealised noble warrior, the same class represented by the war gear of the Hoard. These elite warriors would have helped command in the wars of the 7th century, and it is conceivable the class can be equated with the 30 or so *duces regii* ('royal leaders') that the Anglo-Saxon historian Bede tells us were present in what must have been a large army under Penda

0   20   40   60   80mm

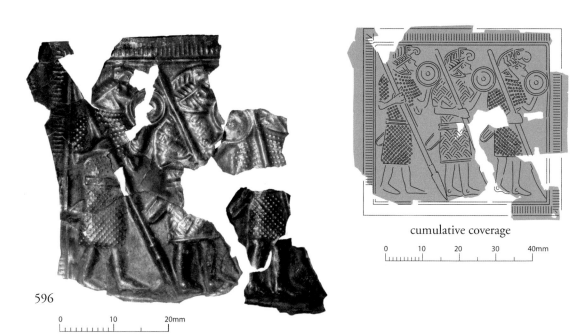

596

0   10   20mm

cumulative coverage

0   10   20   30   40mm

Panels **596–7** from the helmet
with drawn designs.
[Photograph: Cotswold
Archaeology © Barbican Research
Associates; Drawing: C Fern]

in AD 655 (HE III, 24). If every one of the approximately 100 swords
from the Hoard had been the possession of such a leader, prince or king,
then this could mean that the objects represent the warrior leadership of
multiple battles and kingdoms.

Kings were expected to reward loyalty with gifts from the wealth they
achieved by rule and conquest. The giving of golden swords and other
war gear was one means. Another form of expressing fealty was by the
'sword-ring' custom, which developed in Frankia from the 5th century.
Pairs of linked metal rings were at first attached to hilts, usually to the
pommel, to symbolise the inextricable bond of warrior service. Later the
rings were cast 'fixed', and in a final manifestation were knob-like. There
are just three silver sword-ring attachments (**79–84**) in the Hoard, which
must have originally fitted three (probably silver) pommels, additional to
which are three silver pommels (**75–7**) with double ring-knobs that are

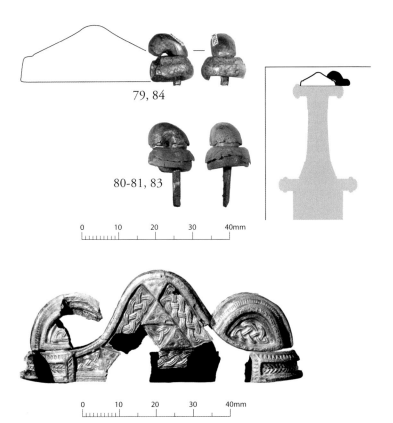

79, 84

80-81, 83

0　10　20　30　40mm

Sword rings **79/84** and **80–1/3**.
[Cotswold Archaeology ©
Barbican Research Associates]

Pommel **75** with ring knobs.
[Cotswold Archaeology ©
Barbican Research Associates]

0　10　20　30　40mm

instances of the ultimate form of the custom. They are unique in having
a pair of 'rings' apiece: no other sword hilt from anywhere in Europe has
two sword rings. Possibly this resulted from a particular circumstance
in which warriors were required to express allegiance to two leaders or
territories. History records several such situations during the formation
of the Anglo-Saxon kingdoms in the 7th century, including when Mercia
had north and south constituents, and the creation of Northumbria by the
unification of two areas, Bernicia and Deira.

The rank and file of the early Anglo-Saxon army may be represented
by the band showing a procession of figures, smaller in scale than the
noble warriors, which ran around the base of the helmet cap (**593**). The
near nakedness of the figures need not be taken literally, but importantly
they are without helmets or mail and appear to be running, or are perhaps
kneeling in fealty. The weaponry of this class is frequently found as iron
spearheads and shield parts in graves: the round shields were of wood
with leather covers and had an iron boss centrally covering a hand-grip.
Many were probably painted (though we have no surviving examples
of patterns) and in rare instances the boards had metal animal mounts.
Most popular were birds of prey, like the gilded example together with
a dragon mount from the great shield from Sutton Hoo Mound 1. Iron

0 10 20 30 40mm

spearheads of the period vary, taking angular, leaf- and sword-shaped
forms, with evidence for an increase in size from the 6th to 7th centuries.

Archaeological evidence for body armour is very rare at this period
in Anglo-Saxon England, suggesting few probably possessed such
equipment. The only example of a mail coat from early Anglo-Saxon
England was found corroded into a lump in the Sutton Hoo Mound 1
burial. Only six helmets are known with substantial remains. They vary
from plain iron caps of *Bandhelm* form, like an example from Shorwell
(Isle of Wight), to those from Sutton Hoo and now Staffordshire with
full ornamental coverings. Another form constructed of iron strips,
the *Spangenhelm*, is represented by the iron helmet from Benty Grange

(Derbyshire). While it is possible multiple commanders within an army would have worn helmets, and that caps of hardened leather might also have existed, the highly ornate helmets of the Hoard and Sutton Hoo are thought to have been equivalent to a crown.

Battle

Our sources give little detail of the make-up of armies or of what actually happened on battlefields of the 7th century. Conflict must have varied from small raids and skirmishes to full confrontations, most of which passed entirely without record. Early medieval forces did use both foot and mounted forces, although it is not clear whether warriors of the period actually engaged the enemy on horseback. Most large armies were doubtless composed mainly of infantry. However, burials of horses and harness in early Anglo-Saxon cemeteries, and stray finds of horse equipment, point to a close association between equestrian culture and elite warrior society, suggesting that possession of a steed trained for war was probably also the prerogative of the few. Multiple fittings (**538**, **556–61** and **567–71**) in the Hoard are suggested as possibly from horse equipment.

For the late Anglo-Saxon period there are accounts of the famous Anglo-Saxon 'shield wall', a linear formation of massed infantry with the front-line holding shields overlapped at their edges. It may be that earlier armies also fought in this manner, but perhaps with military commanders on horseback. The size of armies is very difficult to calculate, though it

Reconstruction of mounts **556–61** as saddle-board decorations. [Photographs: Cotswold Archaeology © Barbican Research Associates; Drawing: C Fern)

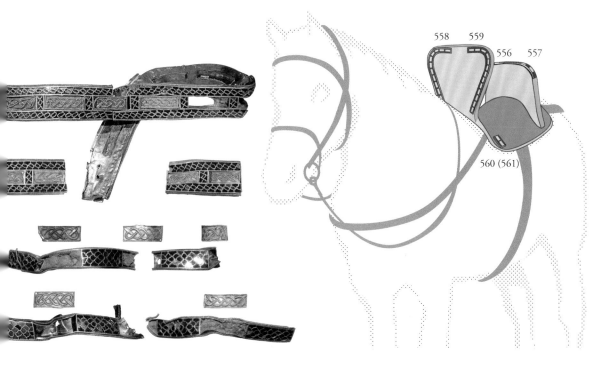

is doubtful that even a very large Anglo-Saxon army of the 7th century fielded more than a few thousand, and most may have numbered only in the hundreds. As already noted, Penda's army in AD 655 might have been such an army. If its 30 leaders on horseback had each commanded an average of 100 men on foot, then it can be speculated that the total size of the force was around 3,000.

Evidence for the use of battle standards is largely lacking, but it is appealing to consider that great cross **539** might have served as one for an army that saw itself as under the aura of the 'cross of victory'.

6 The royal smith

T he Hoard's over 600 objects present almost the full range of techniques and ornament of the early Anglo-Saxon fine metalworker, a class in Anglo-Saxon society that was highly skilled but is poorly understood. Surviving objects provide our main evidence for the methods used, and in this respect the Staffordshire Hoard has contributed more than any find before it. Royal control would have been exercised over manufacture, so the smith was in effect the king's man, producing objects of adornment for both the ruling household and warrior class.

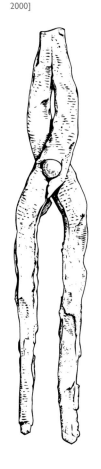

Iron tongs from the Tattershall Thorpe smith's grave.
[redrawn from Hinton 2000]

Smiths and workshops

In British archaeology, only a single actual smith is identified from a 7th-century burial at Tattershall Thorpe (Lincolnshire) from tools, precious-metal scrap and garnets found in the grave. The burial had been placed in deliberate isolation, perhaps because smiths were viewed with suspicion by ordinary society, a caution that was observed even beyond death. The processes required to craft fine metalwork would have appeared magical, even frightening to the majority, requiring fierce temperatures to transform metals and hazardous practices like mercury gilding and quicklime production.

Direct evidence for craftworking includes rare finds of lead models, mould and crucible fragments, and other casting debris and scrap. A number of high-status sites have now produced archaeological evidence, including the royal settlements of Rendlesham (Suffolk) and Sutton Courtenay (Oxfordshire), suggesting further the central control of fine metalworking and precious raw materials. The smithing need not have been limited to a single location, however, as the tools from the Tattershall Thorpe grave show that the equipment was easily portable. A smith might thus have been attached to a royal court as it moved around a kingdom, needing only a dark room in which to forge and cast, so colour changes to flame and metal could be observed, as well as a space open to natural light in which to execute detailed ornament. Whether smiths worked singly or in groups is not known, but it is possible that master craftsmen worked with apprentices. Some objects in the collection have marks to assist assembly, and simpler tasks could have been performed by individuals with lower skill levels, such as the mixing of pastes or the beading of filigree wire. A master goldsmith is recorded in Europe at the time of the Hoard: Saint Eligius (AD 588–660) of the Merovingian royal court of King Dagobert. The Chelles Chalice is attributed to him, and its cloisonné rim has a band of eye shapes that can be closely compared with mounts **542–3**.

LE CALICE DE CHELLES

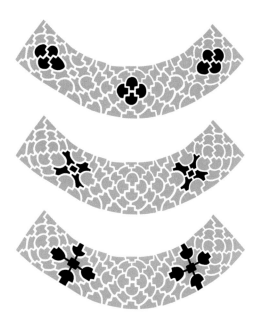

Historic illustration of the Chelles Chalice, lost during the French Revolution.
[The History Collection/Alamy Stock Photo]

One of the pair (542–3) of eye-shaped mounts in garnet cloisonné.
[Birmingham Museums Trust]

Crosses hidden in the
cloisonné of the eye-shaped
mounts.
[C Fern]

Weland

The Germanic legend of Weland the Smith was known widely and survives in multiple works of literature and art. His great deeds supposedly included the crafting of a mail shirt that was given to Beowulf in the epic poem of the same name, and he is depicted on the 8th-century Franks Casket, a small box of carved whalebone that is now in the British Museum.

    The legend tells that Weland was forced to work for King Niðhad, who had him made lame and imprisoned on an island. However, the smith took his revenge by murdering the king's sons and seducing his daughter. The scene on the casket shows him making a cup from the head of one prince, while he hands a drugged goblet to the princess, before making his escape on wings fashioned from bird feathers. The tale reflects that the semi-magical abilities of smiths were indispensable to rulers, yet cautions against mistreatment of the class.

Weland as shown on the Franks Casket.

[C Fern]

Raw materials

The gold used to make the objects was mainly imported in the form of coinage struck in Merovingian Europe, which was in turn recast from Byzantine coinage that had travelled from the Eastern Roman Empire via tribute payments or trade. The Byzantine coins, called *solidi*, were of high fineness gold (typically above 95 per cent by weight [wt%]), but scientific analysis has established that the gold alloys of the Hoard objects are mostly less fine. Of 130 objects examined, the majority were found to be 66–88 wt% gold, with silver and copper making up most of the remaining metal. This is close to the fineness of alloys used in contemporary European and Anglo-Saxon coinage. However, there are a handful of objects, including some of the most exceptional (eg **57**, **370**), with a higher fineness (90–8 wt% gold), much closer to the purity of Byzantine *solidi*. It is possible these items were made for particularly important patrons directly from rare stores of the eastern coinage. A similar gold fineness has been established for the shoulder clasps from Sutton Hoo, objects that are among the closest parallels for the finest cloisonné of the Hoard. A *solidus* was also set at the centre of a cross pendant from Wilton (Norfolk).

    Gold appears to have been relatively scarce in England until a decade or so before AD 600, when it seems there was a sudden increase of the metal flowing from the Byzantine Empire to the west. This period of abundance that is so clearly manifested by the Hoard was short lived, however. By the AD 640s/50s, Anglo-Saxon gold coinage shows considerable debasement by the addition of silver (ie leading to a reduction in gold fineness), suggesting attempts to extend dwindling supplies.

    The stylistically late group of silver hilt fittings in the collection (eg **73–7**, **188** and **409**) may have been made around this date: they show a clear desire for ostentation but with a sparing use of gold details and gilding. That their gold mounts were predominantly set on just one side

Wilton cross (Norfolk) with
a Byzantine coin at its centre
of Heraclius and Heraclius
Constantine (AD 613–32).
[Trustees of the British Museum]

may suggest, furthermore, that each hilt had a specific 'display side'. Silver, unlike gold, was possibly mined in Britain at the time, although imported silver objects were probably also recycled into new objects.

The third major material is garnet, a translucent deep red stone, which was widely used as an inlay in early medieval fine metalworking. For the Hoard objects alone, thousands were cut to shape and inlaid into metal cell-work patterns in the cloisonné technique, though the largest stones are bulbous, cabochon gems, like those with the great cross (**539**). These large gems were probably cut in the Byzantine east and imported, but the small flat garnets must have been shaped by Anglo-

Pommel **73** in silver with a gold
mount and garnet setting.
[Cotswold Archaeology ©
Barbican Research Associates]

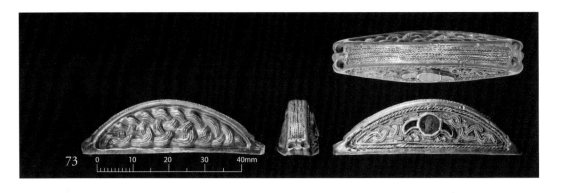

73 0   10   20   30   40mm

Cabochon garnets from great cross **539**, one of which had been broken and repaired.
[Birmingham Museums Trust]

Millefiori inlay on **541**.
[Birmingham Museums Trust]

Saxon craftworkers to fit their geometric or zoomorphic designs. Recent scientific analysis studying the origins of the stones has suggested that most probably came from India, Sri Lanka and the Czech Republic, though exactly how they travelled to England is poorly understood.

In contrast to the dominance of garnet, only a small number of glass inlays occur, typically as single settings, including in the form of millefiori with chequered patterns. One example, unusual for its large size and cabochon form (as the other inlays are flat), is that atop mount **541**. The raw material for glass working at this period in the British Isles was probably recycled Roman scrap or imported glass cullet. Other rare inlays are of rock crystal (pommel **77**), amber (hilt collars **157–8**), and bone (**565**). In addition, a number of pommels (eg **43**), hilt collars (eg **166**) and pyramid fittings (**578–9**) have a degraded, tinged-green substance filling their cloisonné ornament. Despite scientific analysis, it has not proved possible to establish what this decayed material was, though it was definitely a deliberate inlay, possibly originally a brightly coloured enamel or mineral.

Manufacture

The sheet metal that was used extensively for the objects would have been
beaten flat from cast ingots produced from the melted coinage or scrap.
The decoration on the silver sheet of the cap of the helmet (eg **593–7**)
was then impressed using bronze dies (ie stamps) before gilding. The gold
sheet used for the pommels and cloisonné objects was cut to shape and
soldered together. Wire for making gold nails and rivets, as well as the
thin wire that was the basis for the delicate gold filigree, was also made
from sheet, starting as thin strips cut from edges that were then rolled.

Filigree is the most common decoration. In many cases, including
on over 40 pommels, it covers the whole object, though others have only
small panels with the ornament or gem settings with collars of filigree
(eg **539–40**). The technique has a long history traceable to the Greek
and Roman world and was common and widespread across Europe at the
time of the Hoard. Hilt collars **109–10**, each showing a pair of interlacing
quadruped (four-legged) creatures, display the most variations of
technique and pattern, and must have been the work of a master smith.

Cloisonné is another technique with a long history that gained
popularity, in the form of garnet jewellery, across Europe in the centuries
prior to the Hoard. Possibly this was due to a desire to emulate similar
elite jewellery styles in use in the Byzantine world. The garnet analysis
project identified that the peak of garnet cloisonné in Anglo-Saxon
metalworking during the first half of the 7th century occurred at a time
when its use in continental Europe had already declined, possibly due to

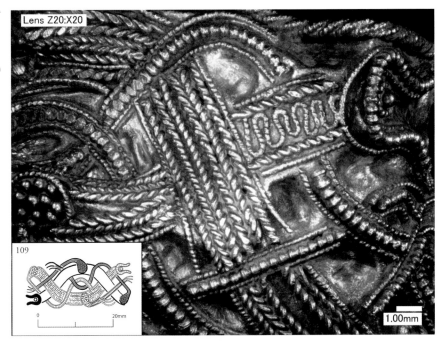

Hilt collar **110** with zoomorphic ornament and (inset) the almost identical design seen on its pair (**109**). [Birmingham Museums Trust; Drawing C Fern]

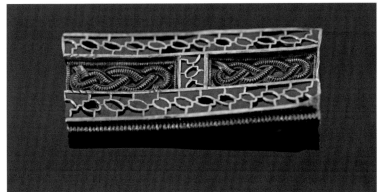

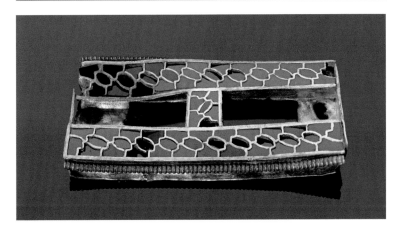

Filigree snake panels set in strip mount **560**, and its pair **561**, shown before its panels were refitted by conservators. [Birmingham Museums Trust]

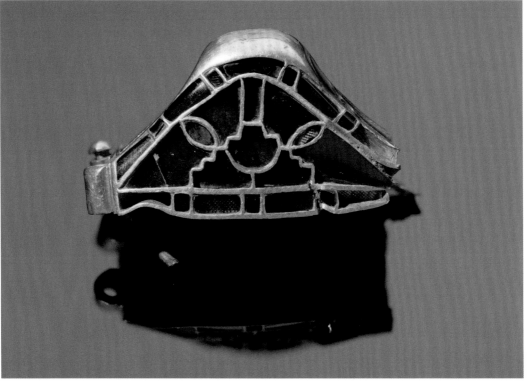

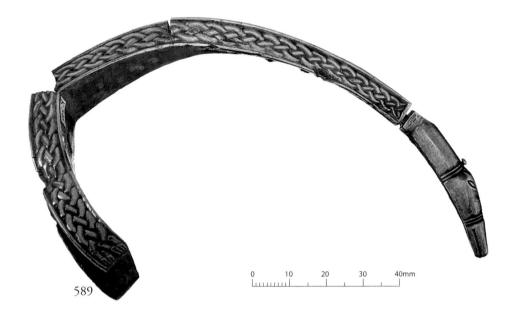

589

0   10   20   30   40mm

a dwindling supply of the mineral. In England, sources of the precious stone must have remained available at least to the mid-7th century (but by what means is unknown). Anglo-Saxon objects, in particular items from Sutton Hoo and the Staffordshire Hoard (eg seax **55**, **167–9**, **225**), rank among the finest examples of the craft known from anywhere in the early medieval world. Nevertheless, more than one cloisonné workshop is indicated for the Hoard objects, since not all examples are so accomplished. For instance, pommels **37–40** and **43–4** indicate altogether less expert execution. Other cloisonné pommels compare closely with examples from Scandinavia, however, as well as with that on the Sutton Hoo sword.

The damaged objects have also revealed other details of construction. The delicate gold-sheet pommels were strengthened with interiors of copper alloy, wood, horn or paste (or combinations thereof), and hilt collars and hilt plates could have linings too. The paste fillers were of lime plaster or beeswax, sometimes mixed, and similar paste filled the base of the helmet crest. Pastes combining wax with animal or plant glue were used in the cells of the cloisonné. A few tiny balls of pure beeswax discovered during conservation seem also to have been included with the collection at burial, probably accidentally, which suggests possibly and intriguingly a direct association between the metalwork and a workshop context prior to burial.

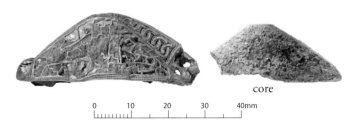

core

0   10   20   30   40mm

Surface enrichment

One key scientific finding was that the gold sheet used to make the objects had been routinely and deliberately 'surface enriched' to improve the gold appearance of the alloyed metal. We do not know the exact method used by Anglo-Saxon smiths, but it required treating the surface of the metal with a weak corrosive substance of some kind to chemically remove some of the silver from the alloy, resulting in a higher gold content at the very surface. On some filigree objects a contrast was created between enriched backplates and untreated ornamental wires, thus helping to make their complex designs stand out.

For comparison, other Anglo-Saxon objects from the British Museum were also analysed, with similar results, proving that the practice must have been widespread. The technique is recorded in later medieval manuscripts, and it is also attested in other cultures worldwide, but it is the first time it has been demonstrated in Anglo-Saxon metalworking.

0   10   20   30   40mm

Pommel **31** has surface-enriched backplates, but its wires were left untreated to enhance the appearance of the interlace design.
[Cotswold Archaeology © Barbican Research Associates]

Under a microscope, layout marks on mount **410** are visible where some of the filigree scrolls have been lost.
[Birmingham Museums Trust]

Lastly, some of the gold sheet objects show fine lines for the laying out of patterns (eg **410**). However, the clearest assembly programmes are those of line and cross marks scratched on the reverse of the small filigree panels that had been inserted into the large cloisonné strip mounts (eg **558–9**).

S3700 20.0kV 50.6mm x10 OTHER1   5.00mm

Marks relating to assembly on strip mounts **558–9**.
[Photo: Cotswold Archaeology © Barbican Research Associates; Drawing: C Fern]

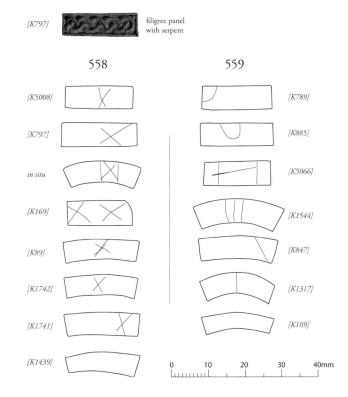

[K797]

filigree panel with serpent

558

559

[K5008]

[K797]

in situ

[K169]

[K89]

[K1742]

[K1741]

[K1439]

[K789]

[K885]

[K5066]

[K1544]

[K847]

[K1317]

[K109]

0   10   20   30   40mm

Overall, a fascinating picture has been revealed of a network of producers and makers, from beekeepers to master smiths, drawing on a range of materials from local beeswax and horn to much rarer gold and garnets that arrived via long-distance trade. Furthermore, as the number of master smiths is always likely to have been very limited, it is possible, if not likely, that related treasures in the collection were produced by the same royal workshops managed by once-renowned individuals, just like Eligius.

7 Belief in the Anglo-Saxon world

I n AD 597, King Æthelberht of Kent, then the preeminent ruler of the Anglo-Saxon kingdoms south of the Humber, received a mission sent by Pope Gregory the Great to convert the English to Christianity. The conversion process was far from immediate, however. Mercia was only converted after the death of Penda in AD 655, and Sussex and the Isle of Wight were the final regions to be Christianised in the AD 680s. There are also many instances from history and archaeology that show a reluctance to relinquish entirely the customs, legends and beliefs that had gone before. Ultimately, many pre-Christian elements of Anglo-Saxon social and intellectual culture remained integral to the fabric of society, as is shown perhaps above all by the example of the pagan god Woden featuring as an ancestor in the genealogies of Christian Anglo-Saxon kings.

Paganism

The pagan religion of the early Anglo-Saxons is poorly understood, due largely to a lack of descriptive sources, but what evidence there is shows some similarity with the beliefs of other northern and central European peoples, including in the gods worshipped. The gods Tiw, Woden, Thunor and Frig are named in the days of the week (Tuesday, Wednesday, Thursday and Friday), and their names also appear in placenames, such as Wednesfield ('Woden's field') in the West Midlands.

Christian writers, like Bede, were little concerned to document pagan custom, but as well as recording Woden, probably the chief deity, as a royal ancestor, certain other important traditions are mentioned. Most significant are Hengist ('stallion') and Horsa ('horse'), named by Bede as the mythic warrior founders of the Anglo-Saxon peoples (HE I, 15). It has been argued that their horse names might indicate that a horse cult existed in pre-Christian England, perhaps associated with the horse sacrifice that was occasionally a feature of pagan burial practice. The animal art on metal artefacts, like that in the Staffordshire Hoard, is now seen as a further, tangible heritage of Anglo-Saxon paganism. It has long been overlooked, because it is very difficult to interpret, but the motifs that recur hint at a wealth of gods, heroes and stories.

Gods and monsters

The myth of Hengist and Horsa tells of the founding of the Anglo-Saxon people by two brothers, who led an army drawn purportedly from the continental tribes of the Saxons, Angles and Jutes, which was invited to serve in the defence of Britain by the leader Vortigern. Its earliest surviving version is in Bede's *Ecclesiastical History* (HE I, 15), but it is highly likely the legend had its origin earlier in oral and possibly cult

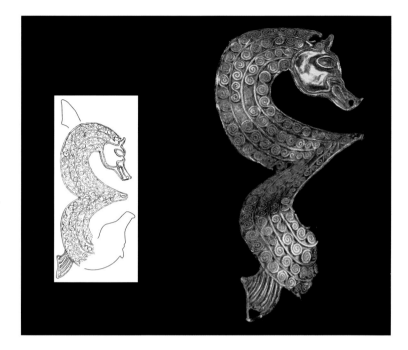

tradition. Bede wrote further that Hengist and Horsa were descended from Woden, and that Hengist was believed to be an ancestor of the kings of Kent. That the names of the brothers are those of horses can also be linked with the importance of horse-riding culture to elite identity in early England. The art of the Hoard also includes many examples of pairs of animals, some of which can be interpreted as horses. Furthermore, a feature of much Germanic animal art is the depiction of shapeshifting human-animal forms. Though fanciful to us, the Anglo-Saxons and other Germanic peoples truly believed in the existence of such supernatural entities, and it is not impossible that the brothers named 'stallion' and 'horse' were once similar in meaning.

On one side of pommel **68** from an imported Scandinavian sword is a bearded head with wide ecstatic eyes, perhaps Odin, the Scandinavian equivalent of Woden. The head is flanked by two disembodied legs, while on the pommel's other side are strange creatures and the heads of boars, a beast that has been suggested as a symbol of royal power. Originally, the silver pommel was part gilded, and its details were highlighted with black niello inlay. It shows considerable wear and may be from a weapon that was long in circulation, very possibly an 'heirloom' sword.

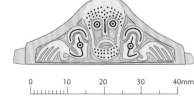

| 0 | 10 | 20 | 30 | 40mm |

Small silver pommel **71** with cast animal heads and incised beasts with biting jaws (not to scale). [The Potteries Museum & Art Gallery, Stoke-on-Trent]

The pair of strange creatures, each with a single leg and back-turned head, between the boar heads on pommel **68** are just one example of the fantastical monsters that abound in the Hoard. Known to art historians as zoomorphs, they are especially common on the filigree objects. Strange beasts and monsters are also a key part of the *Beowulf* legend, including Grendel, Grendel's mother, and the dragon.

Pairs of birds are another common motif in Germanic animal art that has resonance with the image of Odin's ravens, Huginn and Muninn, described in later Scandinavian mythology. Sometimes the god is shown between the birds, as on a small cast silver mount of the Viking period from Lejre (Denmark). The stylised birds depicted in the Hoard have raptorial beaks like birds of prey, however, and some were certainly intended to be eagles, such as those that hold the fish on mount **538**. The eagle was likely a symbol of victory, just as it had been displayed on the military standards of the Roman army.

Birds of prey on mounts **463**, **468** and **536**. [Cotswold Archaeology © Barbican Research Associates]

463   468   536

0   10   20   30   40mm

Christianity

Christian worship was already present in Britain when pagan Anglo-Saxon communities were established. Christianity remained the religion of the Britons in the north and west of the British Isles, and small Christian communities may have survived elsewhere. The Welsh poem 'Marwnad Cynddylan' ('The Death Song of Cynddylan') refers to 'book-holding' monks near Lichfield in Mercia, probably in the 7th century (Rowlands 1990, 174–89). Roman, Frankish, Irish and possibly British clergy were all involved in the gradual conversion of the pagan Anglo-Saxons to Christianity. Bede's *Ecclesiastical History* relates that in the first instance it was the social elite that adopted the new faith, with Christianity thereafter a vital component of Anglo-Saxon kingship and power.

The Book of Durrow, a gospel manuscript of the mid- to late 7th century.
[The Board of Trinity College Dublin, MS 57 f.192v]

The new faith also generated a flourish of artistic endeavour, which prior to the discovery of the Hoard was demonstrated above all by a number of famous manuscripts, including the books of Durrow, Chad and Lindisfarne. Now the Christian objects of the Hoard, not least the great cross (**539**), inscribed strip (**540**) and headdress mount (**541**), attest

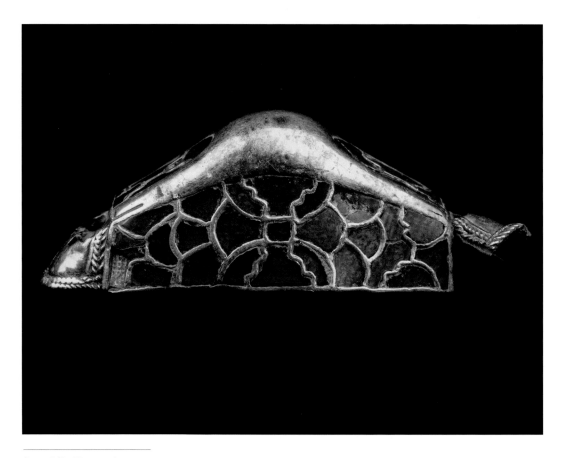

Pommel **41** with a cross in cloisonné (not to scale).
[The Potteries Museum & Art Gallery, Stoke-on-Trent]

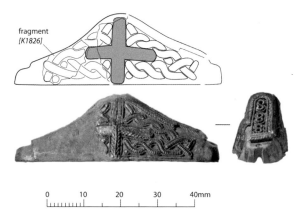

fragment
[K1826]

Pommel **63** with a cross in silver filigree.
[Photograph: Cotswold Archaeology © Barbican Research Associates; Drawing: C Fern]

0   10   20   30   40mm

that the first generations of newly converted rulers were also engaged in the patronage of prestige metalwork destined for religious communities or to serve on the battlefield. As stated, the mount from a processional cross (**539**) shows probably how the cross was adopted foremost by Anglo-Saxon rulers as a symbol of victory: as a powerful talisman that ensured protection and success. In this sense, Christ can be seen to have followed on from Woden as a 'god of war'. In Bede's *Ecclesiastical History*, the same motif of the 'cross of victory' is demonstrated by the account of King Oswald's raising of a monumental cross before the battle of Heavenfield (Northumberland) in AD 633/4 (HE III, 2), following which the Northumbrian ruler defeated a Welsh-Mercian army led by Cadwallon and Penda.

Old and new symbols

In its use of both pre-Christian and Christian symbolism, the art of the Hoard offers an important contemporary record of the conversion. It attests that in this time of great intellectual change, objects were 'canvases' on which makers and users could express both traditional and new ideas. Crosses of various form were incorporated into interlace, animal and geometric patterns, in both filigree and cloisonné techniques (eg **41**, **63**). Not all need to be read as Christian, since the cross as a universal symbol can also be found in non-Christian contexts, but certainly in the setting of the conversion some must have been so. Their occurrence alongside animal art is interesting, in particular, as the style is very likely to have still had pagan meaning.

Historical sources suggest similarly a time of religious flux and syncretism (the combining of different beliefs). Especially well known is the account of the religious practice of King Rædwald of East Anglia. He was baptised at the start of the 7th century AD, possibly with King Æthelberht of Kent as sponsor, but Bede records with horror that shortly afterwards he set up altars both to Christ and to pagan gods (HE II, 15).

Pommel **52** in gold and garnet cloisonné is a most ingenious expression of syncretism. On one side is depicted a pair of fighting beasts that are confronted with entangled limbs. It is just one example of this popular motif known from the Hoard and elsewhere, which has been suggested as representing fighting stallions, and which calls to mind therefore the mythological brothers, Hengist and Horsa ('stallion' and 'horse'). At the ends of the pommel are the curved beaks of birds of prey. The design and meaning are firmly Germanic and pagan. The other side of the pommel, in contrast, carries a design that is Roman and Christian. The architectural style of the rounded and triangular arches that dominate the geometric cloisonné may be drawn from representations in Byzantine art of the Church of the Holy Sepulchre in Jerusalem, which housed the true cross (one example can be seen on the weight illustrated). Correspondingly, at the pommel ends were small cross-shaped garnets. Hence, on this pommel from a sword are symbols both old and new, which might have been considered in combination to offer spiritual protection and the prospect of triumph to the weapon bearer.

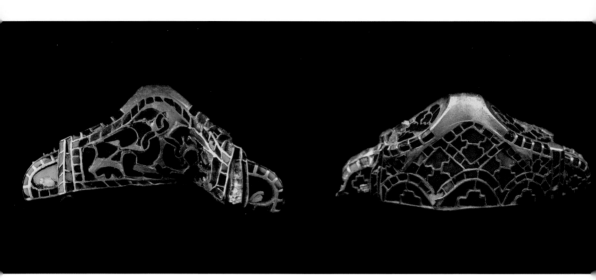

Obverse and reverse of pommel **52** and a drawing of a Byzantine weight of similar date in the British Museum. The weight shows the Church of the Holy Sepulchre in Jerusalem, a similar motif to the pommel design. [Photograph: The Potteries Museum & Art Gallery, Stoke-on-Trent; Drawing: C Fern]

52

'cross' in *arrow* cellwork

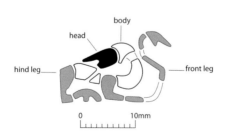

head
body
hind leg
front leg

Byzantine weight
(BN 1985.1015.2)

8 Christian objects

T he rich historical narrative telling of the conversion of Anglo-Saxon kings and of the miraculous lives of Anglo-Saxon saints is only rarely reflected in material artefacts. The Christian objects in the Hoard now provide an unparalleled insight, as sumptuous as it is unique, of the prestigious treasures of the early Church.

Christian conversion

Conversion to Christianity during the 7th century brought new technologies and advantages for rulers. The literacy of the new religion allowed the authority of law codes, reinforced the legitimacy of ruling kings and their families by the recording of king lists, and enshrined territorial holdings by the documenting of land charters. Church building in stone, in contrast to Anglo-Saxon timber construction, saw a return to a mode not seen since Roman Britain. Both these new buildings and the new religious leadership required suites of valuable objects to celebrate the Christian rituals carried out within.

In spiritual terms, above all, during the kingdom wars of the 7th century, it was the power of Christ in battle that was sought. In this, the conversion of Anglo-Saxon rulers mirrored that of the Roman elite before them. In AD 312, Constantine the Great famously saw a vision of the Christian cross before a great triumph in battle. The message was clear: Christ and the cross promised victory. Bede was certainly drawing a parallel in his account of Oswald of Northumbria raising a large cross prior to his victory at the battle of Heavenfield in AD 633/4 (HE III, 2).

Reconstruction of the great gold cross **539**, showing how it might have looked originally.

[C Fern]

Church artefacts

The great cross (**539**) was originally decorated with six large gems, possibly all cabochon garnets. Originally it would have stood about 30cm tall with its jewelled cross and Latin form undoubtedly in the fashion of late Roman and Byzantine processional crosses. However, its design was also influenced by Germanic tradition, since at the ends of the arms

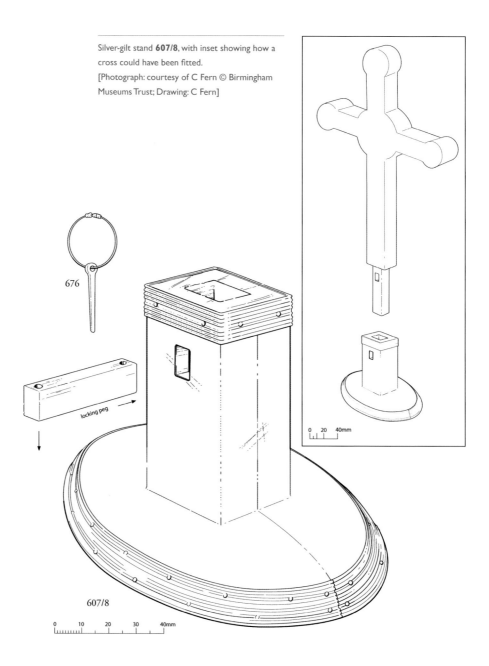

Silver-gilt stand **607/8**, with inset showing how a cross could have been fitted.
[Photograph: courtesy of C Fern © Birmingham Museums Trust; Drawing: C Fern]

676

locking peg

607/8

0 10 20 30 40mm

are lobes similar to those seen on Byzantine crosses, but which uniquely take the form of jaunty animal 'ears' that are proud like those of a horse. The flat body of the cross was made of gold sheet, into which was incised animal interlace, the ornament of the pre-Christian age. Among so much war gear, seeing the cross as a mount for a battle standard is irresistible – an object that would have been known to the Anglo-Saxons as a *sigebeam* ('victory cross') – but the silver-gilt socketed stand (**607/8**) from the Hoard, which is an approximate fit with the cross, suggests it might also have been used as an altar cross when not needed for war.

The Roman tradition of the jewelled cross (*crux gemmata*) that was the model for the Hoard cross is vividly brought to life in the Anglo-Saxon poem *The Dream of the Rood*, in a description that bears striking comparison to cross **539**:

> The portent was all covered with gold; beautiful gems appeared at the corners of the earth and there were also five upon the cross-beam … Magnificent was the cross of victory … I observed that the tree of glory, enriched by its coverings, decked with gold, shone delightfully. Gems had becomingly covered the ruler's tree … I observed the urgent portent shift its coverings and its hues; at times it was soaked with wetness, drenched by the coursing of blood, at times adorned by treasure.
>
> (Bradley 1982, 160)

A D-shaped setting for a gem almost identical to that at the foot of cross **539** is flattened and missing its stone at one end of the folded gold strip bearing Latin inscriptions (**540**). On this evidence, it is possible, if not probable, that the strip was made in the same region and perhaps even the same workshop as the great gold cross and, furthermore, it too might have come from a large cross. Each side of the strip has a similar inscription, although with variations in spelling, abbreviation and spacing. The primary inscription on the obverse reads:

> *Surge, domine, disepentur inimici tui et*
> *fugent qui oderunt te a facie tua*

Gold strip **540** with Latin inscription.
[C Fern]

> Arise, O Lord, and may your enemies be torn apart and
> those who hate you will flee from your face. (Trans. Prof. R Gameson)

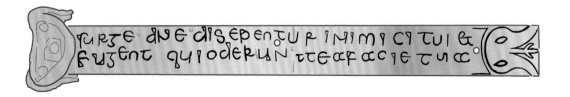

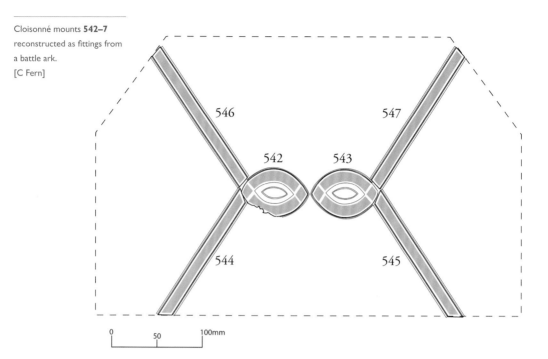

Cloisonné mounts **542–7** reconstructed as fittings from a battle ark.
[C Fern]

546   547

542   543

544   545

0   50   100mm

It is an excerpt, adapted slightly, from the Old Testament, Numbers 10:35, and its belligerent tone fits at once a military purpose. Both great cross **539** and strip **540** can be dated to around the mid-7th century, making the inscription the earliest example in metalwork from England, as well as very similar in date to text in the earliest manuscripts, such as the Book of Durrow, with which its letter forms can be closely compared. The Hoard strip was most likely the work of several people: a goldsmith might have copied the text that was first written out by a literate monk or priest, but the discrepancies between the texts on the obverse and reverse also suggest drafting by different clerics, educated in different traditions.

Additional to these two objects, some of the sets of cloisonné strip mounts may have adorned items such as gospel books or other religious furniture. Mounts **562–4** were designed to fit along the edge of a thin wooden board, possibly the jewelled cover of a manuscript. The reconstructed layout of mounts **542–7** suggests that they could have been attached to the side of a reliquary or some form of portable 'battle ark'. Surviving parallels for these types of object are extremely rare, so the interpretation of the Hoard objects remains tentative.

Personal effects

The cross pendant (**588**) is one of the few items of actual personal costume, which might have been worn around the neck by a religious figure or other prominent Christian. Its equal arms with expanded ends,

Cross pendant **588**.
[The Potteries Museum & Art Gallery, Stoke-on-Trent]

Pectoral cross of St Cuthbert.
[© Chapter of Durham Cathedral]

just over 6cm in total width, are decorated with filigree scrollwork and surround a central, round cabochon garnet. One arm has been bent upwards and another was snapped off, perhaps done as a deliberate act to 'break' the power of the object when it became part of the Hoard. During conservation, the possible arm of a smaller cross pendant (**680**) was also discovered with a sliver of wood inside. This could be a holy relic, as so-called pectoral crosses of the medieval period were often designed to hold such items. No such remains were found at the centre of cross **588**, though it does have a void behind its central garnet.

Headdress mount **541** and an interpretation of the illustration from the *Codex Amiatinus*, showing the prophet Ezra wearing a similar headpiece.
[Photo: Birmingham Museums Trust; Drawing: C Fern]

A small number of other ornate cross pendants of 7th-century date are known from England. The most famous is St Cuthbert's cross, discovered in his coffin and now displayed at Durham Cathedral. It is also in gold and garnet with a small void space possibly for a relic behind its central stone. A recent example of another high-status cross was excavated at Trumpington Meadows (Cambridgeshire), discovered with the 'bed burial' of a young woman. It had been stitched to a garment at chest level and it shows how the wearing of such crosses was not confined to male clerics.

Finally, the unique mount (**541**) in gold and garnet cloisonné has incised animal art closely related to that of the great gold cross (**539**), while hidden in its overall composition are numerous cross patterns. It has fixing holes to allow it to be attached to a base, probably of leather and textile, and it has been identified as the mount from a Christian headdress. It would again probably have been worn by a significant cleric, such as a bishop. The case for it being such is based on a depiction of the prophet Ezra wearing a similar headpiece in an early 8th-century Bible from Northumbria, known as the *Codex Amiatinus*.

Treasures of the East Anglian Church?

Research on the Hoard's small group of Christian objects has pointed to the possibility that several – the great cross (**539**), inscribed strip (**540**) and mount from a headdress (**541**) – could have a single origin (along with other objects), possibly in East Anglia. All are of the highest quality and must represent the commissions of a ruler or rulers within a narrow timescale, probably the second quarter of the 7th century. At this time, the nascent Anglo-Saxon Church attracted rapid and enthusiastic investment from convert kings. Before the Hoard, this had been recognised mainly in terms of the foundation of religious institutions or from the rare survival of manuscripts. Bede records that in East Anglia, kings Sigeberht (AD 630/1–*c* 640) and Anna (*c* AD 640–54) were especially devout and it is probably in their reigns that Christianity was firmly established in the kingdom, supported by religious figures such as Felix and Fursa, including by the foundation of a school for the teaching of letters and a monastery at Cnobheresburg (possibly Burgh Castle, Norfolk). Furthermore, both kings were killed in battle by Penda of Mercia, suggesting one manner by which such superb objects might have travelled to the West Midlands region, in the form of battle loot.

9 Art styles

An abundance of miniature, sophisticated patterns and motifs decorate the Hoard objects. Various forms of ornament occur, mostly interlace, geometric or zoomorphic schemes, some familiar from the period but others less so. The designs were purposefully composed to convey meaning and status, though at the same time often they are deliberately cryptic. Each must be intimately inspected and decoded, yet knowledge of how to 'read' the complex styles could have been restricted, for reasons of power, to the smiths that created them and the ruling class that were the users of the ornate objects. Any special, even sacred, meaning might, by such means, have remained hidden except to the few. Or it may be that the mental effort needed to interpret the message of the ornament was part of a more widespread trend. For instance, puzzling and amusing riddles were an important part of Anglo-Saxon literature. By examining the deeper meaning of the designs and symbols of the Hoard, therefore, we can try to get closer to understanding the Anglo-Saxon mind, and to ultimately consider how such design complexity could have related to religious beliefs.

In addition, the art styles are important for helping to establish when and where the objects were crafted. Similar object forms, art styles and motifs were used across Europe between the 6th and 7th centuries AD, suggesting a widespread and shared vocabulary of power and belief. Therefore, closely related finds from elsewhere in England and beyond that are well dated can suggest appropriate date ranges for the Hoard metalwork, as well as potential origins. However, it is also the case that the Hoard has provided new insights, in particular concerning the development of animal art in Anglo-Saxon England.

Animal magic

Decorative art composed of animal motifs was a key aspect of elite culture in Germanic Europe in the early medieval period. It survives largely as ornament on metalwork from the 5th to 7th centuries, and to a lesser extent in manuscript illumination and sculpture. The Hoard contains 142 objects that are either decorated with zoomorphic patterns or take animal form, a very significant contribution to the number known previously.

One pair of silver hilt collars (**182–3**) are decorated with an early version of the animal art known to archaeologists as Salin's Style I. Disarticulated limbs, heads and bodies of unidentified animals (ie zoomorphs) characterise the style. Style I went out of fashion in England in the mid- to late 6th century, suggesting that the collars may be the oldest fittings in the Hoard, perhaps from an 'heirloom' sword.

Hilt collar **182** and its Style I
animal art.
[Photograph: Cotswold
Archaeology © Barbican Research
Associates; Drawing: C Fern]

182

0   10   20   30   40mm

Salin's art styles

The styles of animal art that were used throughout early medieval Europe from the 5th century were first
studied by Swedish archaeologist Bernhard Salin in 1904. Salin's Style II features on many objects in the
Hoard. It developed from Style I art around the mid-6th century, probably first in Scandinavia, before it
was adopted in England. The animal art is characterised by influence from another form of decoration
called interlace, and it quickly flourished across Germanic Europe, remaining in use in both pagan and
Christian cultures up to at least *c* AD 650. Recognisable creatures include boars, birds, fish, serpents and
four-legged beasts; however, like in Style I, many forms can only be identified as zoomorphs ('animal
like'). Animals can occur singly, though characteristically they are arranged in rhythmical patterns of
pairs or groups.

Style II animal art on helmet cheekpiece **591**.

[Photograph: Cotswold Archaeology © Barbican Research Associates; Drawing: C Fern]

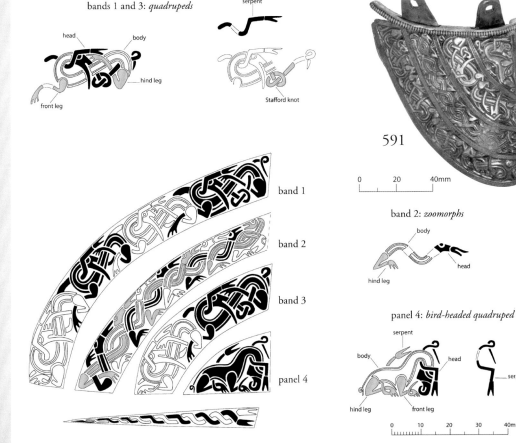

All the other animal-art objects have the ornament known as Salin's Style II (*c* AD 550–*c* 650). The earliest example is silver-gilt pommel **68**, which was probably manufactured in Scandinavia around AD 550. The rest of the Style II objects are Anglo-Saxon, with the designs on the helmet crest (**589–90**) and cheekpieces (**591–2**), great cross (**539**) and seax hilt plate (**567**) now among the finest examples of the art known from anywhere. The style can be deliberately ambiguous, especially the designs in gold filigree, with creatures sharing body parts, or with multiple different readings of beasts and symbols possible. The complex interlace on hilt collar **90** hides a total of 16 zoomorphs formed of looped jaws with

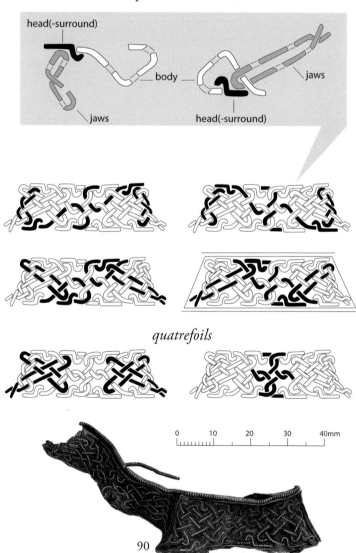

zoomorphs (Anglo-Saxon early Style II)

head(-surround)

jaws

body

jaws

head(-surround)

quatrefoils

0   10   20   30   40mm

Anglo-Saxon early Style II on hilt collar **90**.
[Photograph: G Evans; Drawings: C Fern]

Anglo-Saxon late Style II on great cross 539 (not to scale).
[Birmingham Museums Trust]

90

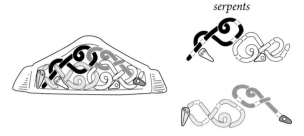

serpents

angled 'head-surrounds' and ribboned bodies. The zoomorphs in the Hoard show the development of Style II in England. Early (*c* AD 570–*c* 630) creatures on filigree pommels and collars are limbless or have hindlimbs but no forelimbs, but during the first half of the 7th century they were overtaken in popularity by the motif of a quadruped shown in profile. Examples of these later forms (*c* AD 610–*c* 650) can be seen in the designs on objects **539** and **589–92**.

Serpent motifs in the Hoard include the four interlacing on pommel **2** with eyes formed of granules of gold. Highly unusual are the three moulded pairs of gold snakes with writhing bodies (**527–32**), the purpose of which is uncertain as they have no parallels: possibly they come from the grips or scabbards of swords, although some Roman helmets had similar cast snake ornament. The helmet crest (**589–90**) and cheekpieces (**591–2**) have complex serpent interlace, too, while the cloisonné mounts (**556–61**), possibly from a war saddle, include over 20 serpent panels in filigree. Possibly the serpent intended was the adder (*Vipera berus*), a species widespread in Europe and Asia, which for its rapid venomous strike might have been thought to bestow a latent but potent form of protection. Serpents can be found in both pagan and Christian symbolism, though in the latter case the creature is typically associated with evil.

Birds of prey, identified by their curved beaks, are a persistent theme in Germanic animal art. The striking pair of birds flanking a fish on large mount **538** were cut from thick gold sheet, into which was carved

Pommel **2** with serpents.
[C Fern]

Serpent mount **527**, one of six in the Hoard (not to scale).
[Birmingham Museums Trust]

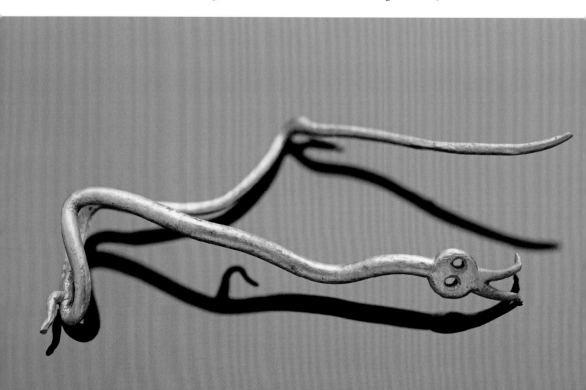

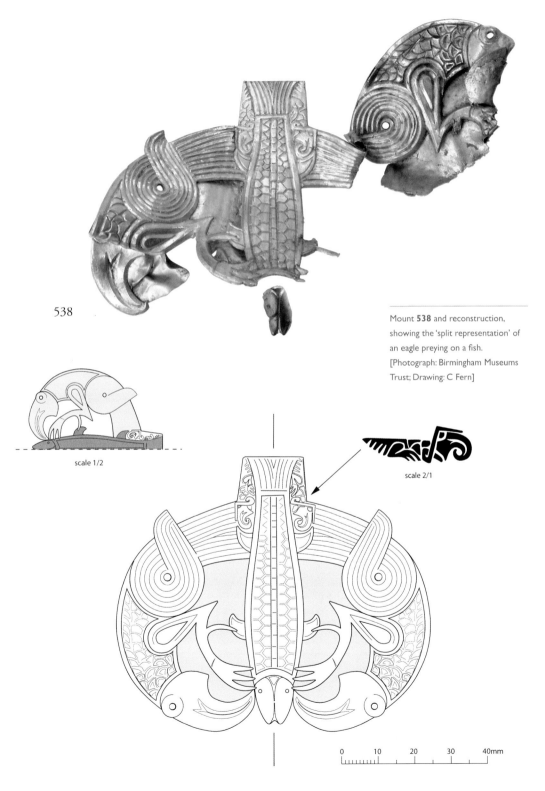

538

Mount **538** and reconstruction,
showing the 'split representation' of
an eagle preying on a fish.
[Photograph: Birmingham Museums
Trust; Drawing: C Fern]

scale 1/2

scale 2/1

0   10   20   30   40mm

Helmet crest **589–90** decorated with serpent interlace, and with animal-headed terminals. [Photographs: Birmingham Museums Trust; Drawings: C Fern]

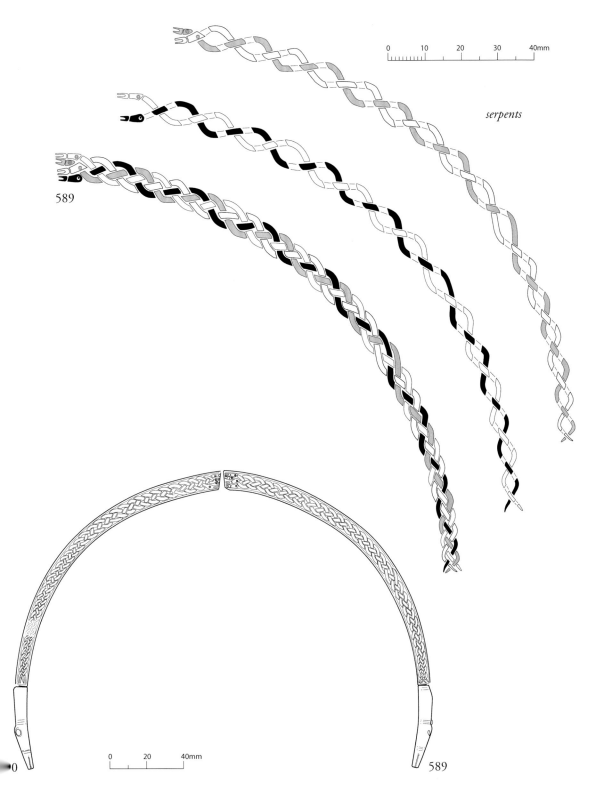

serpents

589

589

Mount **459** (not to scale).
[The Potteries Museum & Art
Gallery, Stoke-on-Trent]

feather and wing detail. However, the design is more complex than it first appears. The fish is double-headed and a line divides its body, indicating an example of 'split representation', a design principle that is seen in many cultures worldwide: by mentally folding the design in half along the division, it was intended to represent two sides of a single bird and fish, thus adding a sense of three-dimensionality. The mount must have ornamented a sizeable flat surface, such as the front of a shield or saddle, war gear that points to a warrior of the highest social order, a prince or king. Other examples of fish with birds include gold mount **459** and the set of three cloisonné mounts (**511–13**) (see p 24). In England, the raptor species most likely to take fish are the sea eagle and osprey, one of which was therefore the likely model.

Pommel **57**, with its lavish cast-gold form and highly unusual animal art, similarly suggests a weapon made for an exceptional patron. The design on both sides is almost identical, with 14 beasts and birds represented in all. Fierce wolf heads are at each end, though most fascinating are the heads of boars either side of the pommel apex that are depicted wearing helmets. This is a playful reference to, and reversal of, the famous motif of the helmet with a boar crest, as described in *Beowulf* and attested by the actual helmet discovered at Benty Grange (Derbyshire).

The fittings from the seax (**55**, **167–9**, **225**) rank close to the finest regalia from the Mound 1 burial at Sutton Hoo (see pp 5, 27 and 47). In

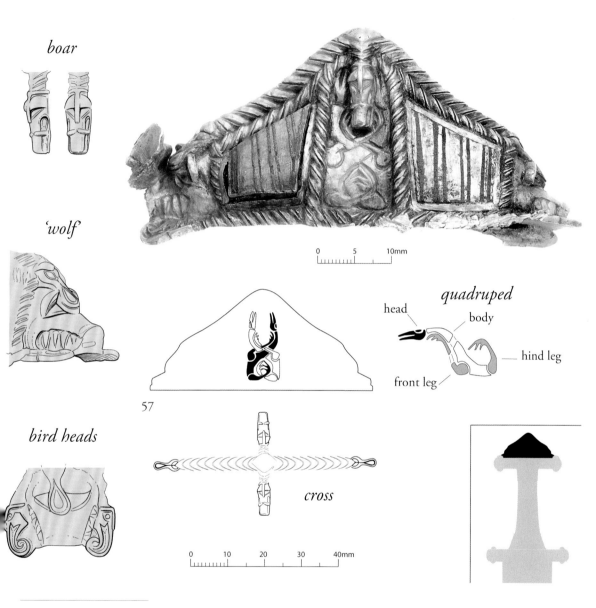

boar

'wolf

57

bird heads

quadruped

head

body

hind leg

front leg

cross

0   5   10mm

0   10   20   30   40mm

Pommel **57** from a 'princely'
sword.
[Photograph: G Evans; Drawings:
C Fern]

particular, the fittings are a match for the finesse of the animal interlace
executed in cloisonné on the Sutton Hoo shoulder clasps. Together they
are exemplars of an Anglo-Saxon style that breaks free of the geometric
patterning of most cloisonné of the period. The animal quadrupeds in
garnet have looping, entwined bodies and limbs, as well as tiny, beady
glass eyes. However, their forms are stylistically slightly later than the
procession of beasts seen on the Sutton Hoo shoulder clasps. Rather, they
can be seen as the forebears of the earliest Style II animal interlace seen in
manuscripts, such as the Book of Durrow (*c* AD 650–80).

The Style II of the cloisonné seax fittings compared with forms from Sutton Hoo and the Book of Durrow (not to scale).

[C Fern]

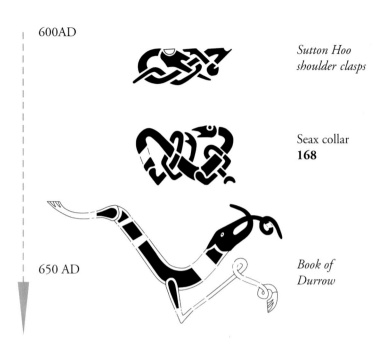

600AD

Sutton Hoo shoulder clasps

Seax collar **168**

650 AD

Book of Durrow

Early Insular style

The latest objects in the Hoard are silver fittings from swords – pommels (**75–7**), collars (**188**), guards (**409**) and pyramids (**580–1**) – grouped by their similar use of gold mounts that were typically applied on one side of the object only, and by their style, which combines Anglo-Saxon and Celtic influences. Known as Insular art, such ornament is characteristic especially of early manuscript illumination, as seen in the Book of Durrow. However, the Hoard metalwork shows an earlier phase of the art, dating from *c* AD 630, so the ornament has been termed the 'Early Insular style'.

The style features cast, tightly woven interlace, as well as Celtic forms including triskelions, triquetras and peltas, uncommon in early Anglo-Saxon metalworking, while the animal art seen on the objects is also unusual. It is suggested, therefore, that the fittings were manufactured in a region or regions that were exposed to a mix of cultural influences – resulting from the coming together of Anglo-Saxon and British workshops and smiths. The border territory of Mercia was one such place in the 7th century AD, but similar conditions might have existed too in British territories taken over by Anglo-Saxon kingdoms, one being Rheged, which was conquered by Northumbria during the 7th century.

Celtic zoomorphic triquetra from pommel **76**.
[C Fern]

Sword pyramid **580** in Early Insular style.
[Birmingham Museums Trust]

Mushrooms, scrolls, knots and crosses

Other Hoard objects have intricate designs of interlacing strands, knots and loops without animal elements. Some patterns are regular, like the interlace seen in Roman art, while others are irregular, an ornament of Germanic invention and perhaps favoured for its writhing serpentine quality. The most complex of these designs look at first meaningless, like that on gold filigree pommel **33**, but careful deciphering in this case shows a dense and deliberate tangle of three strands. The appeal of interlace for past cultures is believed to stem from such complexity, which could even be perceived as a means to magically ensnare or confuse evil forces. In this way interlace and animal interlace may have acted like an amulet to bring fortune and protection.

Regular filigree (zoomorphic) interlace on pommel **1** and irregular filigree interlace on pommel **33**. [Cotswold Archaeology © Barbican Research Associates; Drawing: C Fern]

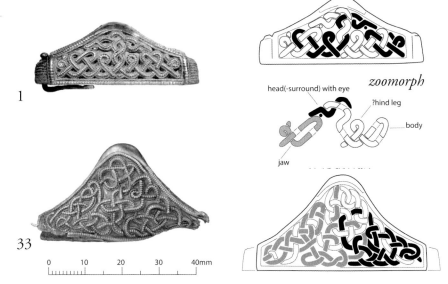

Gold filigree scrollwork is especially common on the small mounts from the grips and guards of sword hilts (eg **438**). This form of decoration is very old, reaching back to at least the 3rd millennium BC. Filigree scrollwork is also seen on other early Anglo-Saxon metalwork, especially on the so-called plated disc-brooches of the kingdom of Kent, manufactured in the decades either side of AD 600.

The majority of the cloisonné objects are decorated using a style of stepped and repeating geometric patterns also found in Merovingian Europe. Numerous garnet shapes were used to create the recurring patterns, most of which are found on objects outside, as well as within, the Hoard. One in particular, the 'mushroom' (also found as a half-mushroom shape), features especially among the cloisonné regalia of Sutton Hoo, as well as on other finds from East Anglia, such as the Wilton cross. Occasional rare finds with mushroom forms are known from elsewhere in England and Europe, but this particular association is notable as it points again to the possible manufacture of part of the Hoard

Filigree scrollwork on mount **438** (not to scale).
[The Potteries Museum & Art Gallery, Stoke-on-Trent]

Mushroom cell-work on hilt collar **162** (not to scale).
[Birmingham Museums Trust]

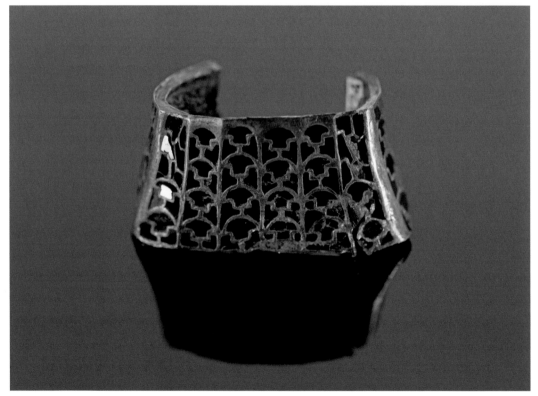

within the kingdom of East Anglia. The Sutton Hoo and Wilton cross parallels, the latter dated by its Byzantine coin, suggest together that the related Hoard cloisonné dates to *c* AD 610–50.

Crosses also occur in the cloisonné ornament as small cut garnets (eg hilt collar **178**) or formed within patterns. Those in patterns include quatrefoil arrangements of mushroom and arrow forms that may, like the

Garnet cross on hilt collar **178**.
[Cotswold Archaeology ©
Barbican Research Associates]

Filigree mount **462** shaped like
a fish.
[Birmingham Museums Trust]

animal art, have been deliberately cryptic. On eye-shaped mounts **542–3**, three crosses can be read, standing for the crucifixion (see p 58). A very similar arrangement notably occurs on pommel **47**(see p 45), which must therefore be from the same workshop. There is no doubt that many of these symbols were Christian in intent, although it is also the case that crosses (or quatrefoils) can be read in some of the filigree animal art, including formed by the serpents on pommel **2** (see p 86), objects which very likely predate the conversion.

The fish is another well-known Christian symbol, so the fish-shaped filigree mounts (**461–2**) may have been possessions of followers of the new faith. However, it also occurs in earlier pagan animal art in England, and especially when combined with other creatures (eg mounts **459** and **538**) a pre-Christian meaning probably pertained.

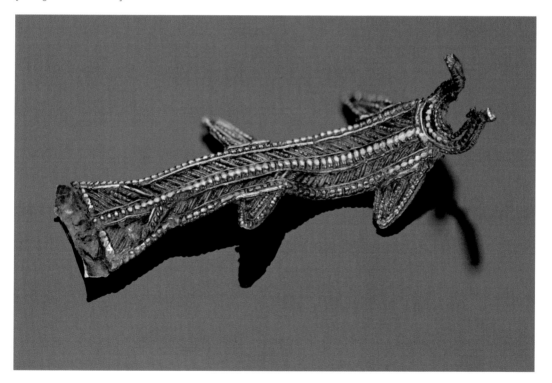

10 Treasure of kingdoms

The kingdoms of early Anglo-Saxon England emerged only gradually during the 6th and 7th centuries. Their first beginnings and that of their royal houses are murky, but for the 7th century we are better served, thanks largely to Bede's *Ecclesiastical History*. The dynasty most visible to us in archaeology is that buried at the cemetery of Sutton Hoo. The burial ground founded late in the 6th century is thought possibly to have been that of the royal line of East Anglia, the Wuffingas. The treasures found in the ship burial under Mound 1 show us how important it was for rulers to control precious resources, such as gold and garnet, as well as to harness the skills of the smith who could transform them into jewels and regalia bearing pagan and Christian iconography.

The ability to successfully hold and expand territory, yielding resources, trade and strong relations with other regional and foreign rulers, was crucial to the survival of an Anglo-Saxon king and kingdom. It is clear from the high number of kings killed in battle in the 7th century that a ruler was expected to be an active warrior, and the cost for failure was high. Military reputation was doubtless important to gaining the following of the warrior class that dominated society, but sustained kingly power was dependent too on maintaining a royal treasury from which rewards to supporters could be granted. In *Beowulf* we meet the archetype of a ruler in King Hrothgar, who draws generously on a store of fine weapons, armour and regalia, as well as a stable of warhorses, to reward the hero Beowulf.

Penda (c AD 626/33–655)

Penda of Mercia was one of the most powerful rulers of his day. His reign, starting in 626 or 633 and lasting over a quarter of a century, was characterised by unrivalled success in war that led ultimately to the emergence of the Mercian kingdom. While no direct link between him and the Staffordshire Hoard can be proven, the collection of war gear from defeated kingdoms and its date range correspond with Penda's warlord career.

Bede's *Ecclesiastical History* portrays Penda as the pagan scourge of the newly Christian kingdoms of East Anglia and Northumbria, describing him as 'a most warlike man' (HE II, 20). The Mercian ruler killed no fewer than five kings from these two regions, including at the battles of Hatfield (AD 633) and Maserfelth (AD 642), before he was defeated and killed by Oswiu of Northumbria at the battle of Winwæd in AD 655.

Penda's father is named as Pybba, the earliest common ancestor of four dynastic lines. Mercian kings claimed descent from the peoples of Germanic Europe, as other Anglo-Saxon kings did. However, there was probably considerable British influence within the ethnically mixed Mercian region. Indeed, Penda's name might derive from the Celtic *pendevic* or *penndav*, meaning 'leader' or 'chief-most', and his first alliances were with Welsh kingdoms. Nor is it correct to see Penda as an intolerant pagan, since even Bede admitted that he did not forbid Christianity within Mercia (HE III, 21).

In the Hoard we can recognise, in a way not possible before, the true extent of the valuable material assets of the early kingdoms of England – chiefly the unprecedented array of gold-hilted swords manufactured in royal workshops as rewards for the warrior class. In addition, the collection presents us with 'princely', even 'kingly', objects, including the helmet and possible war saddles. It is tantalising, of course, to think that King Penda of Mercia *might* have collected and controlled such a treasure, won as battle loot from his noted victories. His long and successful reign coincides with the date of the Hoard, though nothing can be connected certainly with any historical ruler or other figure, nor can we say who was responsible for its burial. But with confidence it can be stated that the collection must attest to the existence of a significant 'central person', in archaeological terms, in the Mercian heartland at the time of the kingdom's rise during the early 7th century.

Kingdom styles

The different ornamental traditions represented by the Hoard's sets of hilt fittings in filigree and cloisonné show that swords could have hilts decorated according to prevailing fashions. It is possible these were regionally based, and so several 'kingdom styles' have been suggested for the Hoard metalwork. Developed in royal workshops, they would have signalled warrior allegiance to a ruler and territory, as well as status.

Best represented in the collection is a filigree style, evidenced by gold pommels and hilt collars (eg **1**, **87–8**), with designs of interlace or Style II animal art. Based on their ornament, most were probably manufactured

Hilt fittings (**1**, **87–8**) of the filigree style *c* AD 570–*c* 630.
[Cotswold Archaeology ©
Barbican Research Associates]

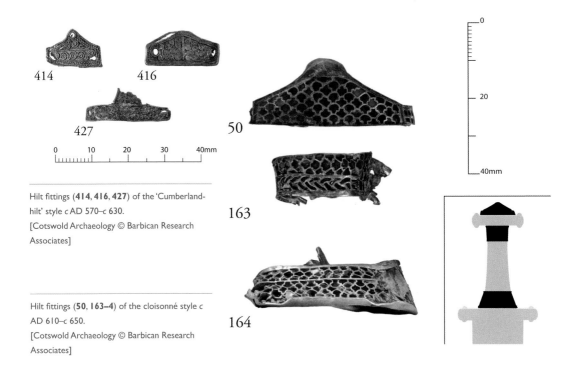

Hilt fittings (**414**, **416**, **427**) of the 'Cumberland-hilt' style *c* AD 570–*c* 630.

[Cotswold Archaeology © Barbican Research Associates]

Hilt fittings (**50**, **163–4**) of the cloisonné style *c* AD 610–*c* 650.

[Cotswold Archaeology © Barbican Research Associates]

c AD 570–*c* 630. Similar filigree decoration has long been recognised as characteristic of brooches and buckles from excavated graves of similar date in Kent and southern England. Since the 1990s, however, a growing number of pommels and collars with filigree have been recorded from across Britain as single finds made by metal detectorists. The most significant is the set from Market Rasen (see p 28), but others are also akin to the Hoard examples. The distribution of these finds (with no examples so far from Kent) suggests possibly that the style had its origin in a kingdom located in the Midlands or the north of England, with the major kingdom of Northumbria a tempting possibility.

The many small fittings from grips and guards that are like those of the Cumberland hilt (see p 33) might represent another style using filigree scrollwork ornament. The 'Cumberland' provenance of the exemplar (in the modern-day county of Cumbria) could indicate that this was also a northern fashion, which it is believed was probably broadly contemporary with the filigree style just discussed. Both might have been followed in the northern region by weapons fashioned in the Early Insular style (*c* AD 630–*c* 660), a style resulting perhaps from the Northumbrian conquest of British territories.

Many of the pommels and collars in garnet cloisonné (eg **50**, **163–4**), including those from the seax (**55**, **167–9**, **225**), have been shown stylistically to be most related to objects that were manufactured in East Anglia. The metalwork of Sutton Hoo shows that this region of England saw a great flourishing of the ornamental technique in the early 7th century. On the evidence of parallels, it has been argued this cloisonné style of hilt furniture dates to *c* AD 610–*c* 650. In addition, on stylistic

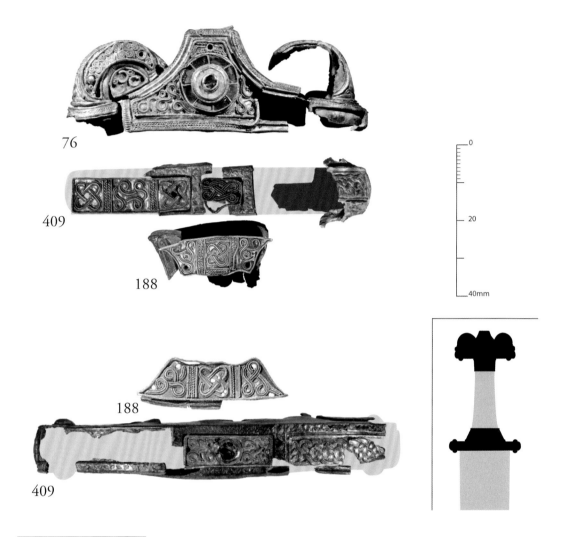

76

409

188

0

20

40mm

188

409

Hilt fittings (**76**, **188**, **409**) of the
Early Insular style c AD 630–c 660.
[Cotswold Archaeology ©
Barbican Research Associates]

grounds, other key objects were also probably produced in the kingdom, including some of the church objects and sets of cloisonné mounts (eg **538–66**). Not all the cloisonné is of a single workshop or region, however: those objects with less expert cloisonné (eg **36–40**), sometimes combined with filigree, may represent the output of a different territory.

A helmet 'fit for a king'

The reconstruction of the helmet from the Hoard has now joined the Sutton Hoo example as one of the most iconic objects of Anglo-Saxon England. The Hoard helmet was found in approximately 1,600 pieces, amounting to around a third of the total fragment count for the whole collection. However, none of the substructure survives – the ironwork, leather and other elements that would have formed the helmet cap onto

Reconstruction of the 'silver'
(tinned bronze) helmet from
Sutton Hoo.
[Paul Mortimer]

Reconstructed 'gold' (silver-gilt)
helmet from Staffordshire.
[Birmingham Museums Trust]

which the fragmented decorative ornament was attached. The making of
a physical reconstruction allowed the decorative scheme proposed by the
research project to be tested, and the possible construction of the helmet
to be investigated.

The Hoard helmet was originally just as impressive as the Sutton Hoo
helmet. However, there are key differences. It would have had a golden
appearance, rather than the silver of Sutton Hoo; it had a nasal instead of
a facemask; it had smaller cheekpieces that were fixed instead of hinged;
and, most impressively, it had an actual crest, probably originally of
horsehair or feathers. Its crested form and decoration with panels and
bands of warrior and animal art relate it not only to the helmet from
Sutton Hoo, but also to helmets from rich graves found in Scandinavia,
notably at the ship-burial cemeteries of Vendel and Valsgärde (Sweden),
as well as, ultimately, to the helmet of 8th-century date from a pit at
Coppergate in York. The size of the Staffordshire cheekpieces suggests
they were set relatively low on the missing iron cap, so the original helmet
might have looked similar in form at least to that found in a 'warrior'
grave at Wollaston (Northamptonshire).

The panels and bands in silver-gilt sheet were impressed with dies
(stamps) and held in place between riveted, reed-patterned strips, so that
they repeat their designs of warriors and animals over the whole helmet
cap. They have been reconstructed as a hierarchical scheme representing
Anglo-Saxon warrior society and perhaps mythologies linked with royal
power. Lowermost, set in a silver band around the base of the cap (above

Iron helmet from Wollaston
(Northamptonshire).
[Museum of London Archaeology]

the cheek-pieces and neck guard) is the rank-and-file procession of small warriors brandishing spears and shields (see p 54). Above them is a band of interlaced quadruped beasts. Over this band are set the panels of marching elite warriors, in bird-crested helmets and mail, shown considerably larger in size as military sub-commanders (see p 52). On both sides they march towards the front of the helmet (meaning two different dies were used). Uppermost are panels with different designs: one shows a victorious figure on horseback (see p 102), representing a king riding down a foe; the other shows two warriors in the act of a ritual dance. These mainly figural panels of the cap present a contrast with the bold animal art of the cheekpieces, crest and neck guard, which may have been linked with pre-Christian pagan beliefs. However, none of this investment of wealth, craftsmanship and iconography prevented the ultimate act of destruction that befell the helmet: before burial, the cheekpieces were forced outwards until their tabs broke, the crest and silver band were levered from the cap, and its silver coverings were peeled off.

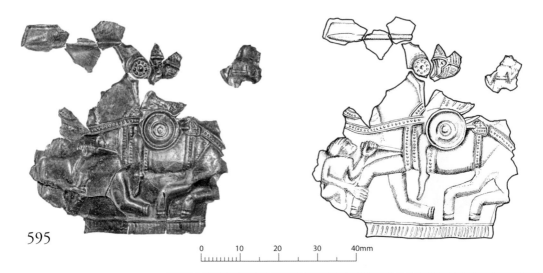

595

0 10 20 30 40mm

Helmet panel **595** showing a horse
rider.
[Photograph: Cotswold
Archaeology © Barbican Research
Associates; Drawing: G Speake]

Making the Staffordshire Hoard
helmet reconstruction.
[Drakon Heritage and
Conservation]

The 'high king's war seat'

The few objects that are thought to come from horse equipment again indicate the possessions of individuals of the highest rank and even royal status. Large gold plaque **538** (see p 87) with its device of a fish and birds of prey was possibly stripped from a grand war saddle, while one set of large cloisonné mounts (**556–61**) might have furnished another (see p 55). In addition, the unusual set of niello mounts (**567–71**) has been interpreted as fittings from a horse bridle (see p 16).

In one episode in *Beowulf*, King Hrothgar rewards Beowulf with eight horses with gilded harness, on one of which was the 'high king's war-seat', a saddle skilfully and richly wrought, we are told. Archaeological evidence has confirmed that an equestrian culture existed among the ruling elite around the time of the Hoard, including rare instances of sacrificed horses with harness found within or near graves containing weaponry and high-status grave goods. Anglo-Saxon armies travelled considerable distances to do battle, although to what extent possession of a trained steed for war was restricted to aristocratic warriors, princes and kings is uncertain. Actual saddle remains of the period are rare, especially from early Anglo-Saxon England. However, examples of 5th- to 7th-century date from continental Europe and Ireland show that a form of saddle existed with high front and back wooden boards, which helped to firmly seat the rider in a time before stirrups.

(i) Mount **538** interpreted as a decoration from a saddle front board, compared to (ii) a reconstructed saddle from Wesel-Bislich, Germany.
[C Fern]

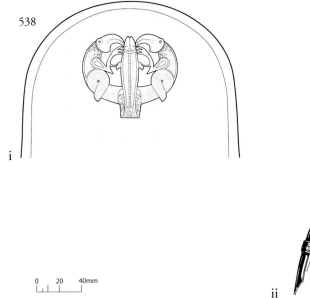

538

0   20   40mm

i

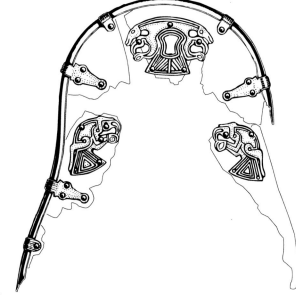

ii

Overall, these and the other rich objects suggest an emphasis on prestigious display. Although many questions remain about the provenance of the Staffordshire Hoard, it seems likely that the elite material came from more than one kingdom, possibly gathered over different campaigns, as well as from political gift exchanges. For the first time, we are able to conceive of the true portable wealth and regional pomp of Mercia and its neighbours in this crucial period.

11 Burial

A brutal end

The Hoard's 4kg of gold was doubtless of high value when deposited, *c* AD 650–*c* 675, yet it is interesting to note that it is dwarfed by contemporary treasures recorded by history, like the 200,000 gold *solidi* (900kg) paid by the Visigoths in the 7th century to the Merovingian king Dagobert I. Its proposed date for burial is based on the latest material, the metalwork of the Early Insular style (*c* AD 630–*c* 660). However, we cannot say, in the absence of any associated archaeological features at the site, what form the burial took, only that the pit (or pits) must have been shallow as nothing survived below the depth of modern ploughing (*c* 30–45cm). Nevertheless, the relationships between the objects, their related styles, groups and sets, as well as the characteristic damage they had suffered before burial, favours the idea that the collection was interred together at a single point in time. Only a single shred of Anglo-Saxon linen was found (with hilt collar **126**) to suggest that a cloth bag might have been the container.

The damage almost every object had suffered was microscopically examined to understand the treatment of the collection in its final stages above ground. Frequent cut marks indicate that knives were used to prise, lever and slice fittings and rivets apart (eg **314**, **456**), while some pommels show dents left by the smithing tongs that were used to pull them from the ends of their weapons (eg **56**). It is most likely that the object breaking and sorting was done by smiths – the same class responsible for object manufacture – as they would have had the tools necessary, as well as the knowledge to separate gold from gilded metal.

56

314

Damage to pommel **56** from tongs and to collar **314** from a knife. [Photographs: G Evans; Cotswold Archaeology © Barbican Research Associates; Birmingham Museums Trust; Drawing: C Fern]

0   10   20   30mm

Slash mark on mount **538**
(not to scale).
[Birmingham Museums Trust]

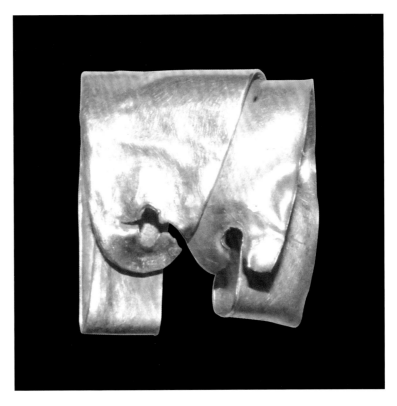

Folded up hilt plate **325**
(not to scale).
[Cotswold Archaeology ©
Barbican Research Associates]

It is clear that the marks are the result of removing the fittings and are not due to battle damage. A small scar on the fish and bird mount (**538**) is perhaps an exception, though even it is relatively light, not like the chopping or stabbing marks that result from sword and spear blows. Few objects were removed intact, so reuse was not the intention. Furthermore, a small number have damage that *might* be considered ritual in character. The clearest example is the broken arm of cross pendant **588**, an act that was possibly done to destroy the Christian power of the object. Other objects were folded, notably great cross **539** and strip **540** with its biblical Latin inscription. However, this could alternatively have been done to fit these larger objects into a small bag or other container, and some other large objects (**544–7**) were also cut up, possibly for the same reason. Additionally, the head of the fish (a Christian symbol) on mount **538** had been removed (see p 87), an act that cannot have been caused by the mount's removal, suggesting again a desire to destroy what was certainly a powerful image.

The purpose of this object breaking (or iconoclasm) is unclear, but the disregard for the exquisite fittings, each a work of art and ideology, is striking. The destruction of the helmet, Christian symbols and elite swords could be interpreted as acts of vengeance against the possessions of the defeated secular and religious commanders of an army or armies. The missing iron blades of the weapons, in such a scenario, could have been quickly re-hilted and put back into circulation, to better equip the victorious army. However, to date, the absence of comparable buried collections from the British Isles indicates that the Hoard does not represent a ritual that was widely practiced, for instance an offering to a pagan war god, though it might be seen as an exceptional, singular such example. Or perhaps its purpose was purely economic, and it represents straightforwardly the precious-metal loot from a victorious battle or series of campaigns that was destined for recycling into ingots or new objects in a Mercian royal smithy, but if so, its route to this end must have been diverted and it was fatefully lost.

A lonely burial?

Somehow, whether interrupted en route to the crucible, or gathered deliberately for another purpose, the collection ended up buried on a hilltop above Watling Street. The absence of any archaeological context for the find means that it is difficult to reconstruct the circumstances of the act of burial. It could have been interred temporarily for safekeeping, it might have been hidden in an illicit act, or perhaps was buried with great ceremony at a place considered special. Its location is both isolated and strategic. The immediate setting was unimproved land, possibly thinly wooded and away from local settlements. But the chosen spot, between two 'folk' groups, was also at the heart of what would become royal Mercia, close to the intersection of the main routes into the kingdom, Roman Watling Street and Ryknild Street. The hilltop setting was also a prominent landmark, perhaps unsuited to a secretive act, but as a location it might easily have been returned to.

Watling Street

The Hoard was buried on a hill next to Watling Street, an important landscape feature that was already ancient in the 7th century AD. It was first used in the Iron Age, and in the Roman period became one of the main thoroughfares of the province of Britannia. It ran from Canterbury (Kent), through London, and all the way to Wroxeter (Shropshire). Watling Street remained a major route in the Anglo-Saxon landscape, and in a 9th-century treaty between Alfred the Great and Guthrum, leader of the Viking Great Army, it formed part of the boundary separating the Anglo-Saxon and Viking realms.

The Roman settlement of Letocetum (Wall), at the junction of Watling Street and Ryknild Street, was located about 4km from the Hoard findspot and probably remained a significant site in the early Anglo-Saxon period.

Roman site of Letocetum, next to Watling Street.
[Jenni Butterworth]

Horse-harness mount **698** is not believed to have been part of the Hoard, as its three fragments were found over 40m away. It is of disc form with a raised saucer rim and was cast in copper alloy with interlace ornament that was gilded. However, its type of interlace is like that seen on the latest objects in the collection (of the Early Insular style), indicating it is contemporary with the date of deposition. It is tempting to speculate, therefore, that it might have been lost from a horse with elaborate harness owned by an individual present at the time of burial.

At the heart of Mercia

The research has shown that each object has a story to tell, from the worn and century-old pommel **68** (and its sword) created for a pagan, Swedish aristocrat, to the freshly crafted cross pendant **588**, probably commissioned for an important Christian cleric. Close study of the objects has provided, in particular, insight concerning the craftspeople that made them. Arguments based on form, function and style coincide to suggest that portions of the collection could have come into Mercia from the rival kingdoms of East Anglia and Northumbria. All were valuable objects of power, seemingly selected and kept in the collection for that reason: the swords of commanders and sub-commanders, the kingly helmet, mounts from saddles and church treasures. Some *might* have been princely gifts, though the treatment of the objects seems to favour that most were the hated war gear of vanquished foes.

If we cannot be sure what brought these items together for burial, it is undoubtedly true that the period in which they were created, circulated, assembled and buried was an extraordinary one. It was a time of endemic warfare that brought about rapid political changes, as well as religious transition with conversion to Christianity. It is impossible not to be tempted by the little we know of Mercian history in the 7th century to align the Hoard with known figures and events. King Penda (c AD 626/32–655) looms large as the most successful military leader of his age, whose victories significantly increased Mercian power and influence over neighbouring kingdoms, including Northumbria and East Anglia. Five rulers of East Anglia and Northumbria were slain in battle by the armies of this Mercian warlord, before he himself was killed in the aftermath of battle. Such events are tantalising, in view of the princely objects the collection contains, but, equally, other recorded battles or accounts of treasure offer possible episodes that we might link with the find. Ultimately, the sparse historical sources for the period do not allow us surety. Far from diminishing the Hoard's interest, however, this uncertainty only increases the appeal of its mystery, of a find without parallel, a treasure of warriors and kings.

Afterword

The Hoard stands as a monument to a critical period of history that saw the formation of Anglo-Saxon England. Its study has transformed scholarly understanding of the production and wealth of the war gear of the ruling warrior class, and of the masterworks of the Christian Church of the 7th century AD. In art-historical terms, its objects have forced a reconsideration of the date of the earliest surviving manuscripts, and possibly of the origin of some.

As a great treasure, the Staffordshire Hoard has captured the popular imagination around the world. At the time of writing, more than two million visits have been made to museum galleries where the collection has been displayed. The publication of the Hoard academic monograph and online catalogue allows access worldwide to a limitless audience. It has generated television programmes, theatre productions, works of art, novels and children's books, even new garden and architectural designs. In an age of financial challenges for archaeology and heritage, the Staffordshire Hoard is perhaps most valuable as an example of the ability of the past to inspire, educate and bring together individuals and communities.

Glossary

Almandine	Type of garnet, a silicate mineral.
Anglo-Saxon	Period of English history from 5th to 11th centuries AD. The Hoard is from what is known as the early Anglo-Saxon period.
Assemblage	Collection of finds.
Beaded	Gold or silver wire worked with a tool to look like a string of beads.
Boss	Decorative knob that typically covered the head of a rivet or nail, or the large iron knob at the centre of a shield which protected the grip and hand.
British (kingdoms)	The western and northern parts of the British Isles.
Byzantine	Culture of the Eastern Roman Empire based on Constantinople (modern Istanbul).
Cabochon	Rounded gemstone, without facets (but sometimes with a flat top).
Celtic	The western parts of the British Isles, particularly used to describe art and culture.
Cloisonné	Decoration formed by a metal cell-work structure, typically inlaid in the period with garnet and occasionally other materials, such as glass.
Conversion	The adoption of Christianity by individuals and political groups.
Copper alloy	Mix of copper and other metals. Most often tin was added to form bronze.
Early medieval	Period of history across Europe from the 5th to 11th centuries AD.

Filigree	Decoration in gold or silver formed of fine wires (often beaded) and granules soldered to a metal back-sheet.
Fineness (wt%)	Measure of gold quality relative to other metals in an alloy, expressed as 'percentage by weight' (wt%). In modern terms, 18 karat gold is 75wt%.
Frankia/Frankish	Region (and culture) roughly equivalent to modern France and parts of Germany from the 3rd century AD.
Germanic	The shared culture and language of ethnic groups in northern Europe in the Greek, Roman and later periods.
Interlace	Decoration composed of looped, braided and interlinked strands or motifs.
Merovingia/Merovingian	Kingdom and cultural period named after the ruling dynasty of Frankia in the 5th to 7th centuries.
Millefiori	Rods of different coloured glass combined lengthways and heated, then sliced, to produce glass 'gems' with patterned designs.
Organic	Materials derived from plants and animals, rather than minerals and metals.
Ornament	Decoration applied to objects.
Pagan	Spiritual belief outside the major world religions, often polytheistic (having many gods).
Pommel	Knob or cap attached to the blade tang, at the end of a sword hilt or grip, often decorated.
Pyrope	Type of garnet, a silicate mineral.
Reliquary	Container for sacred objects, such as the bones or clothing of Christian saints.
Romano-British	Denoting the people and culture of the British Isles under Roman rule (c 1st to 5th century AD), as well as the survival of that culture in regions beyond Anglo-Saxon control after the 5th century.

Salin's Style I/Style II	Decoration featuring animal and human motifs found on metalwork across Europe in the 5th to 7th centuries AD.
Seax	Large knife with a single edge used for fighting or hunting.
Silver-gilt/gilded	Application of a thin surface of gold to silver or copper-alloy metal, to make it appear golden.
Tribute	Payment made by one political or military group to another to avoid war or as demanded as an act of political subservience.
Triskelion	Triple spiral motif with rotational symmetry, a feature of Celtic art.
Vikings	Peoples of Scandinavian origin engaged in raiding, adventuring, trading and settling during the 8th to 11th century.
Votive offering	A deliberate deposit of valuable objects or other offering, made without intention of recovery, for a sacred purpose (eg a gift to a god).
Zoomorph(ic)	Animal-like form that cannot be identified to an individual species, sometimes deliberately fantastical, or an animal body part used as ornament. They are typical in Salin's Styles I and II.

Bibliography

The Staffordshire Hoard is owned by Birmingham City Council and Stoke-on-Trent City Council, and is on display at Birmingham Museum & Art Gallery and the Potteries Museum & Art Gallery, Stoke-on-Trent. The Staffordshire Hoard research project was funded by Historic England and the museums, and the academic monograph derived from the research project is published by the Society of Antiquaries. A full online catalogue of the collection is freely available at https://doi.org/10.5284/1041576, hosted by the Archaeology Data Service.

Barbican Research Associates 2019 *The Staffordshire Hoard: An Anglo-Saxon Treasure* [data-set]. York: Archaeology Data Service [distributor] https://doi.org/10.5284/1041576

Bede *The Ecclesiastical History of the English Nation*. London: JM Dent (1910 edn), available at Internet Medieval Sourcebook, https://sourcebooks.fordham.edu/basis/bede-book1.asp

Bradley, S A J (ed) 1982 *Anglo-Saxon Poetry.* London: Everyman

Carver, M 1998 *Sutton Hoo: Burial Ground of Kings?* London: British Museum Press

Carver, M, Sanmark, A and Semple S (eds) 2010 *Signals of Belief in Early England: Anglo-Saxon Paganism Revisited*. Oxford: Oxbow

Evans, A C 1986 *The Sutton Hoo Ship Burial*. London: British Museum Press

Fern, C, Dickinson, T and Webster, L (eds) 2019 *The Staffordshire Hoard: An Anglo-Saxon Treasure*. London: Society of Antiquaries of London

Halsall, G 2003 *Warfare and Society in the Barbarian West, 450–900*. London and New York: Routledge

Heaney, S 2000 *Beowulf: A New Verse Translation*. London: Faber & Faber

Rowlands, J 1990 *Early Welsh Saga Poetry*. Cambridge: DS Brewer

Williams, G 2011 *Treasures from Sutton Hoo*. London: British Museum Press

Yorke, B 1990 *Kings and Kingdoms of Early Anglo-Saxon England*. London and New York: Routledge

Index

Page numbers in *italics* refer to pages where topics appear in illustrations only.

Tailpiece images overleaf (double page spread) The bearded face on pommel **68**; (top)
Filigree serpent on cloisonné mount **558**; (bottom) Animal art on great gold cross **539**.
[The Potteries Museum & Art Gallery, Stoke-on-Trent]

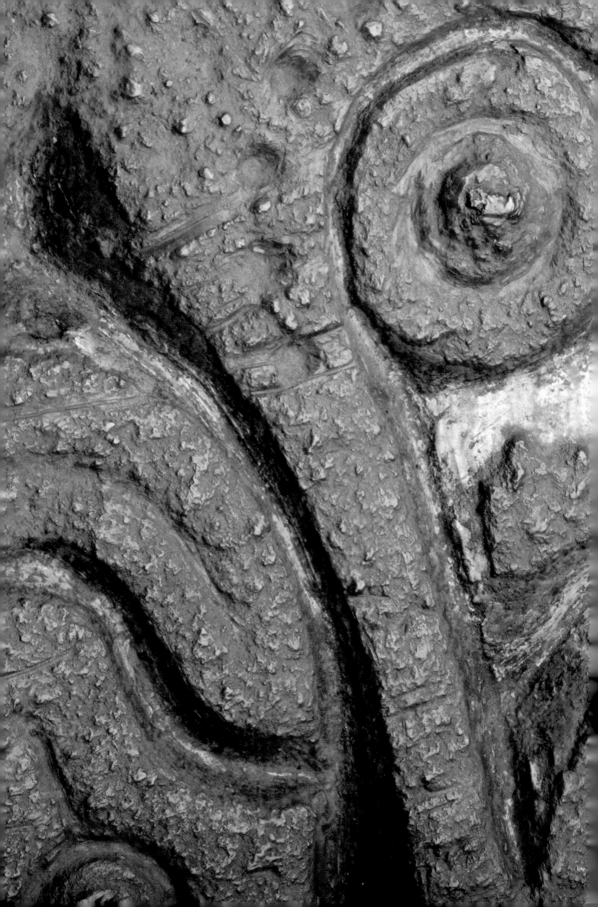

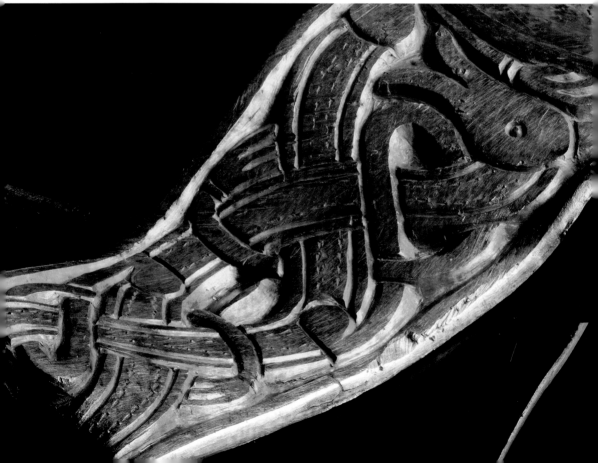